√ 9/93

WOMEN
IN SOCIETY

CHINA
PAMELA TAN

MARSHALL CAVENDISH
New York • London • Sydney

Reference edition published 1993 by
Marshall Cavendish Corporation
2415 Jerusalem Avenue
P.O. Box 587
North Bellmore
New York 11710

© Times Editions Pte Ltd 1993

Originated and designed by
Times Books International, an imprint of
Times Editions Pte Ltd

Printed in Singapore

Library of Congress Cataloging-in-Publication Data:
Tan, Pamela,
     Women in society. China / Pamela Tan—Reference ed.
     p. cm.—(Women In Society)
     Includes bibliographical references and index.
     Summary: Provides a historical overview of the experiences
     of women in Chinese society, discussing their participation
     in various fields and profiling the lives of significant women.
     ISBN 1-85435-556-2
     1. Women—China—Social conditions—Juvenile literature
[1. Women—China.] 2. China—Social conditions.] I. Title.
II. Series: Women in society (New York, N.Y.)
HQ1767.T36 1993
305.42'0951—dc20   92–33354
                                  CIP
                                  AC

Women in Society

Editorial Director	Shirley Hew
Managing Editor	Shova Loh
Editors	Irene Toh
	Vijaya Radhakrishnan
	Goh Sui Noi
	Sue Sismondo
	Maureen Kelly
	Andrea Borch
	MaryLee Knowlton
Picture Editor	Yee May Kaung
Picture Researcher	Sirege
Production	Edmund Lam
Design	Tuck Loong
	Ronn Yeo
	Felicia Wong
	Loo Chuan Ming
Illustrators	Jimmy Kang
	Kelvin Sim
	Li Xiaohong
MCC Editorial Director	Evelyn M. Fazio

Introduction

he recorded history of women in China is one of total repression. However, some 20,000 years ago, there existed a hunter-gatherer society that was matrilineal in organization. Excavations show group burials where women were buried in the center of the tomb, and children were buried with women, not men.

As society developed and settled communities were established, women became subordinate to men. Excavations of later ancient graves reveal the wife's corpse in a bowing position facing the husband. By the 9th century B.C., the patriarchal society was firmly established.

Absolute male dominance has been a feature of Chinese society for more than 4,000 years. Thus, acceptance by women of male dominance is deeply ingrained.

In 1949, the Communist Party of China came to power. One of the party's platforms was, and still is, equality for women. Legally women in China have equal rights with men, and in the large cities in the workplace, among well educated people, women do have equality. However, this applies to only a tiny minority. For the overwhelming majority of Chinese women, there is still much ground to be covered toward achieving equality and eliminating the idea of male superiority.

This book tells you how women have been suppressed and oppressed in China over the centuries and what they have done to change that. It also tells you about Chinese women today, how they live, think and work, and their aspirations and hopes.

Contents

chapter one

The Courtesan

O ur story takes place in 16th-century Beijing, during the Ming dynasty. The capital of China, Beijing was where imperial examinations were held every three years to select government officials from among the country's scholars. Li Jia was one such scholar from Zhejiang province, where his father was the provincial governor. He was a handsome young man and placid in nature.

At that time there lived in Beijing a beautiful courtesan who was famed for her grace, knowledge of poetry, and singing. Her name was Du Wei, but she was known as Du Shi Niang, or the 10th maid, as she was the 10th courtesan to enter the brothel.

When Li Jia and Du Shi Niang met, they fell in love, and for a year they lived together.

At first the mistress of the brothel allowed this, for as long as the young man spent generously she had no complaint. Then, after a year when his money began to dwindle, she started to complain to Shi Niang.

Finally the old woman said if Li Jia would give her 300 taels of silver in 10 days she would let Shi Niang go.

Opposite: A heart-broken Du Shi Niang throwing her treasures into the river.

Right: Du Shi Niang and Li Jia spent a happy year together in Beijing.

Li Jia tries to raise money

Li Jia knew he would have difficulty raising the money as most of his friends shunned him because he spent most of his time in a brothel. Moreover, he had neglected his studies and missed the imperial examinations.

Nonetheless he set out to borrow money. But no one lent him any.

Very depressed, Li Jia went to see an old friend, Liu, to whom he told the story. Liu said this was a ploy to get rid of Li Jia because the girl and her mistress knew he had no more money.

Li Jia knew this was not true, and for the next two days he tried again to borrow money, but to no avail.

When after six days Li Jia still could not raise any money, Shi Niang gave him 150 taels of silver, telling him to raise the rest himself.

When Liu saw Shi Niang's money, he was moved, for this showed she was devoted to Li Jia. He helped Li Jia find the rest of the money, and Shi Niang's freedom was bought.

Li Jia meets Sun

Thus the lovers were married, and they set off on a long journey by boat along the Grand Canal to Zhejiang in the south. Again Li Jia had no money, and Shi Niang took from her jewelry box 50 taels of silver for the journey.

It was November, and the silver rays of the full moon shone on them. Li Jia asked Shi Niang to sing for him, and she did so happily.

Their boat was anchored for the night, and in a boat nearby was a wealthy young man by the name of Sun. When he heard the lovely sound of Shi Niang's singing, he was determined to meet her. He told the boatmen to moor alongside Li Jia's boat. Late that night a huge snowstorm fell that stranded the boats.

Thus Sun was able to catch a glimpse of Shi Niang. He was so enthralled by her beauty that he decided to win her over. He invited Li Jia for a drink on shore. A crafty man, Sun quickly found out the couple's story. Pretending to be greatly concerned, he said, "And what of your honorable family? What will they think when you return with no money, no government position, and with one so lacking in chastity?"

Sun reminded Li Jia that if he separated from his family over a courtesan, he would be considered a person of no virtue, unfit to inherit or look after his father's property.

He then suggested that Li Jia part with Shi Niang. "I will give you 1,000 taels of silver for her, which you can take back to your family. This will make your return easier."

When Li Jia returned to his boat, he found Shi Niang waiting eagerly for him. But he turned his head away and sighed. She questioned him, but each time he tried to speak only tears fell. Finally he told her everything, saying he wanted her approval before accepting the offer.

"Then go early tomorrow and get the money," she said quietly, "and make sure he does not trick you."

Shi Niang kills herself

Early next morning Shi Niang dressed herself beautifully and went on the deck.

Li Jia returned with the 1,000 taels of silver and stood sadly before her, hardly daring to look at her.

She had her jewelry box in her hands, which she unlocked, and from the first drawer took out jade earrings and ornaments worth hundreds of ounces of silver. Then, in front of the astonished Li Jia, Sun and the boatmen, she threw the jewels into the water. She opened a second drawer, full of flutes of gold and jade worth several thousand ounces of silver that she again cast into the water. She opened a third drawer and took out a handful of lustrous pearls and emeralds the value of which none could estimate. These too she threw into the water.

Li Jia, stricken with remorse, tried to put his arms around her, but she pushed him aside and said, "I was a plaything for the world for many years. Little by little I saved up these jewels which I thought would support me in my old age. Then I met you and we swore together an oath of fidelity, vowing never to change.

"These treasures I intended to use so your return home would be splendid and fitting. But what a pity your love is not deep! You have already cast me aside halfway through the journey. I have thrown away these jewels so you may see how paltry in comparison the sum was which you preferred to me. You did not see me as I really was. I despise you!"

Then, still holding the jewelry box, Shi Niang leaped into the water.

Women of China

Du Shi Niang was not representative of the women of her age or even of other courtesans who lived in her time. What she had in common with them was the oppression she suffered, her lack of rights, and the vulnerability of her social position.

Although a courtesan, she dreamed of freedom, of a happy life, and of love, all of which were denied her because of a social system in which women's rights did not exist. She dared to stand up and oppose the system, finally using her death to defy it. She rejected the man she loved, who like many men, perpetrated the system.

This story also describes the life of many Chinese women who are expected to be strong, silent, and long suffering; and that of many Chinese men who are dependent on the family and conform to the norms of society.

Women of China have through the ages lived a life of oppression with few social rights.

chapter two

Milestones

The women of China have played a rich and varied role in the formation of the state, its history and its culture, as well as in its periods of reform and revolution.

One cannot, however, appreciate the role of Chinese women without looking at the historical and social background of Chinese society. Since 221 B.C., China has been a state with centralized authority. The philosophy of this Chinese state has always included male dominance over women.

Confucius, in the 5th century B.C., taught that all women must practice three obediences—obedience to the father before marriage, to the husband after marriage, and to the son after the death of the husband.

Starting in the 11th century, Chinese women had their feet bound—a cruel, crippling practice. In the 17th century, the proverb "a woman's virtue lies in her ignorance" embodied what was expected of women.

A vegetable seller in a free market in Kunming (*opposite*) and a computer technician (*right*). Despite oppression, Chinese women have contributed through the ages to Chinese society in ways large and small.

However, throughout the ages, there have always been outstanding women who have achieved distinction. With the arrival of Western imperialism and the opening up of China, together with Western ideas of liberalism and equality, young women demanded education and civil rights. They felt deeply for China and the humiliating injustices it suffered at the hands of foreign imperialists. Together with their male compatriots many women fought, sacrificing themselves, their sisters and their daughters for a free, prosperous, and democratic China.

Woman washing clothes by the Yellow River. It was on the banks of this great river that a matrilineal society existed 7,000 years ago.

Early history

Excavations show that China was inhabited 500,000 years ago. The country has a 4,000-year recorded history, with the earliest records being inscribed on oracle bones and tortoise shells. The inscriptions are in ancient Chinese characters.

The Chinese who lived along the Yellow River over 7,000 years ago were hunter-gatherers, and evidence shows that the society was matrilineal. Descent was through the woman, and men lived in the homes of their wives. Women were respected, and all children took their mother's name.

Xia dynasty (2100–1600 B.C.)

During the Xia ("shee-ya") dynasty (2100–1600 B.C.) society became more stable. People were no longer hunter-gatherers but farmers. Customs changed and men were now in charge of the family property instead of women. Thus, the position of women began to change. Now descent was traced through the man, and upon marriage women went to live in their husband's homes.

The Chinese had begun ancestor worship; that is, sacrifices were made to ancestors in order to ensure them a happy afterlife. These sacrifices could only be made by male descendants, and this meant that a male heir was necessary to perform the rituals and continue the family line.

Shang dynasty (1600–1100 B.C.)

By the Shang dynasty (1600–1100 B.C.) ancestor worship was well established among the aristocracy and the noble clans. The peasantry had no part in ancestor worship. That was because they had no surnames, nor did they have any land. Marriage customs also differed greatly. When the nobility married, they did so with splendid and elaborate ceremonies. Peasants, however, celebrated a festival in spring in which young men and women from different villages met, paired off and had sexual intercourse. If a girl became pregnant by autumn, she and her partner were married.

During the Shang dynasty, schools were established, but girls were not admitted. Girls from noble families who received education were usually taught by an elder female relative. Some enlightened scholars paid for tutors to teach their daughter at home. However, most girls received "women's instructions," which were taught in the women's chambers. Girls learned cooking, silk and flax weaving, and how to assist in offering sacrifices to gods and ancestors. They also received lessons on conduct, and before they married, they had to learn the four virtues of a wife: morality, proper speech, modesty, and diligence.

Girls from common families learned household skills from their mothers, and they too were instructed to be obedient to their husbands and serve their in-laws after marriage.

Fu Hao: stateswoman, strategist, diviner

Oracle bones record the achievements of Fu Hao, wife of the Shang emperor Wu Ding.

Fu Hao was an outstanding stateswoman and strategist. She presided over sacrificial ceremonies and offerings to the gods—including human sacrifice. She was also a diviner, which at the time gave her political status. As a strategist she played an important part in a series of wars during the reign of Wu Ding.

For her achievements, she was granted land and slaves. She was honored with her own tomb instead of being buried with her husband, the emperor. Objects found in her tomb included bronze vessels, more than 6,000 pieces of jade, and over 7,000 pieces of shell money. There were also the corpses of 16 slaves in the tomb.

Feudal age (1100–221 B.C.)

The feudal age in China is divided into three periods: the Zhou period (1100–770 B.C.), the Qun Qiu ("chun chi-you") period (770–476 B.C.), and the period of the Warring States (476–221 B.C.)

During the Zhou period, Zhou rulers maintained effective control of feudal states strung out along the valley of the Yellow River. The first two centuries saw peace and stability. This was also the time that the patriarchal system was formally established, under which the status of women was greatly reduced. Women who had taken part in politics and military affairs during the Shang dynasty were now ridiculed as "hens crowing at dawn." Under the Zhou dynasty women were deprived of their right to own personal property.

Marriage The Zhou aristocrats initiated a set of laws and rites so the family functioned in the same way as the kingdom. Under the new laws, the father was dominant over the son and the husband was dominant over the wife, just as the sovereign ruled over his subjects. Men and women were separated to prevent adultery: women lived in separate quarters away from the main part of the house, and husbands went to their wives' quarters at night. If adultery occurred, the men were punished by castration and the women were locked up.

The rites established the authority of parents over their children. If parents were not pleased with their daughter-in-law, their son had to cast her out, even if he loved her. If the parents were pleased with the daughter-in-law and their son did not love her, he could not break the marriage. Love had nothing to do with marriage.

The practice of arranging marriages through a matchmaker was established during the Zhou period. This has lasted through the ages and is still widely practiced in the rural areas.

One of the most important marriage rites was the sending of betrothal gifts to the prospective wife's family with an offer of marriage. Betrothal gifts reflected the social status of the husband and wife. The more gifts the woman's family received, the higher the wife's status. Anyone who could not afford betrothal gifts had to live with his wife's family and work for them. The practice was called using labor instead of money to get a wife.

Officials in charge of marriages had to order men to be married by 30 and women by 20.

The main duty of a wife was to have sons to continue the family line. She had to respect her in-laws, care for them and other older family members, and spend most of her time on domestic chores. It was in the parents' interest to select a meek and servile daughter-in-law.

A man could take more than one woman, but only one of them was recognized as a wife. The other women were designated as concubines and they were treated as little more than slaves.

Divorce Wives could not initiate divorce, but it was very easy and common for husbands to divorce their wives in the Zhou dynasty.

The husband's family would send a person to the wife's family to tell her parents, "Your son-in-law said it is his fault that he can't eat with your daughter anymore. He asked me to tell you this." The woman's parents would say, "It's our fault. He should do as he sees fit." The marriage would thus be over.

Wives could not contest a divorce. They had to endure whatever their husband and his family meted out to them.

Male superiority is established Male superiority and female inferiority were firmly established during the feudal period. The ancient *Book of Changes* (*I Ching*) established the theoretical grounds for this. It was stated in the book that the success or failure of a family depended upon the woman, and that the woman's place was in the home, while the man's was outside.

Women could not inherit family property. Property went to the wife's elder brother or to her eldest son. The sons of the concubine had no inheritance rights. If there were no sons, the property went to a male member of the clan.

A Zhou emperor in the women's quarters. It was during the feudal period that the status of women was greatly reduced.

> Wives are acquired through ceremony. Elopement yields mere concubines.
> —The Book of Rites

Confucius' teachings had great impact on women which is still felt today.

Confucius In the 8th century B.C., the Zhou dynasty disintegrated into seven separate states, thus bringing on a period of anarchy and violence. This period, from 722 to 481 B.C., is known as the Qun Qiu or Spring and Autumn period.

It was also a time when Chinese philosophy flourished.

Only women and petty men are hard to deal with. If you come close to them, they are no longer respectful. If you keep them at a distance, they become resentful.
—Confucian Analects

Confucius lived during this period of turbulence. A scholar, he traveled from state to state seeking a prince who would listen to him and put his ideas into practice.

Confucius' teachings were meant to combat what he saw as the decaying morals of the times. He emphasized filial piety (devotion of sons and daughters to the parents) and loyalty to the ruler, and opposed the individualism and anarchy that were prevalent.

Confucius' beliefs stressed the importance of right behavior. Everybody, from the king to the ordinary subject, must behave correctly. In the family and in society, each and everyone had his or her own place and must perform the duties of that position. The old must care for the young, the young must respect the old, the ruler must look after his subjects, and the subjects must respect and obey the ruler. Only when this happened would there be peace and harmony.

Confucius found little support for his teachings during his time. Later, however, emperors used his principles to educate people and rule the state. From the Han dynasty until the Qing dynasty, a period of more than 2,000 years, only men well-versed in Confucian studies could enter government service. Over the centuries, Confucianism has molded not only the Chinese character, but also the Chinese people's way of thinking.

The Han dynasty historian Ban Zhao, in her book *Precepts for Women*, set down the way women should behave as women, as mothers, and as wives, according to Confucian principles. These rules still form part of the outlook of many Chinese women today and influence their behavior.

Qin dynasty (221–206 B.C.)

The Qin ("chin") dynasty marked the beginning of a centralized China as we know it today. The man responsible for unifying China was a Qin king who called himself Qin Shi Huang, or "the first emperor." During his reign Confucius' books were burned and Confucian scholars buried alive. Qin Shi Huang was ruthless and he was determined the whole of China would come under his rule. His concept of a unified China under one powerful centralized rule has lasted until today.

Qin Shi Huang not only unified the country, he also unified the political system and standardized weights and measures, the monetary system, and the written language. It was at this time that the Great Wall of China was built. Previous states had built many sections of the wall to defend themselves from the raids of the Xiong Nu, a nomadic people living in the north. Qin Shi Huang launched a grandiose project linking the pieces together into what is now known as the Great Wall. Hundreds of thousands of men were conscripted

into building the wall, during which many died.

The emperor also demanded a common set of customs and moral values. One of his edicts stated: "Men should be satisfied with their work in the fields and women should be content with their duties in the home."

He ordered the common people of other states he had conquered to "uphold decency" and "refrain from licentious behavior." He encouraged widows to remain faithful to their deceased husbands and not to remarry.

> No one is to be punished for killing a woman who has become pregnant out of wedlock.
>
> —*Qin Shi Huang*

Temple of Meng Jiangnu. Meng Jiangnu lived during the Qin dynasty. Her husband was one of many men forced to work on the Great Wall. When she heard that the place her husband went was very cold, she made some warm clothing and then traveled hundreds of miles alone to the north. But her husband had died and was buried in the Wall. She cried so hard with grief that part of the Wall collapsed, revealing her husband's grave. She jumped into the grave to join him in death.

Han dynasty (206 B.C.–A.D. 220)

The Han dynasty (206 B.C.–A.D. 220) succeeded the Qin. The Han grew into a very powerful imperial state. Han rulers revived the doctrines of Confucius for their political needs. Confucius had taught the obedience of sons to their parents, of the nobles to their lord, and of the lords to the emperor. The Han rulers expanded the obedience of the lord to the emperor to include all subjects of the empire.

Confucian teachings gradually became the doctrine of the entire society. It was during the Han dynasty that strict moral guidelines were formally and systematically encoded. The three cardinal rules of the society were—the ruler guides his subjects, the father guides his son, and the husband guides his wife. For women, the notion of "virtuous and obedient wives" took root, as such virtue was rewarded—faithful widows could expect grain or cloth, or memorial arches by their tombs on their death.

The historian Liu Xiang ("lee-you see-ang") and later the woman historian Ban Zhao ("pan ja-oh") laid down rules on female decorum that eventually became known as the three obediences and four virtues (see pages 11 and 13). These increased the moral fetters in which women were placed.

Marriage and the law Another development in the Han dynasty was the laying down of seven grounds for casting off a wife; previously a man could turn his wife out of his home whenever it suited him. These grounds included not bearing a son, being licentious, not waiting on her mother-in-law, nagging, stealing, showing jealousy, or contracting an incurable disease.

However, there were also three circumstances under which it was forbidden to divorce a wife—if the wife had no relatives to support her, if the wife had observed the three-year mourning period for the death of a parent-in-law, or if the man had been destitute when he married her.

Ban Zhao in her study. A historian who lived during the Han dynasty, she wrote the *Precepts for Women* which set down the standards for their behavior.

Political marriages

The Han court also practiced political marriages, in which princesses or noblewomen were married to the chiefs of neighboring tribes in order to keep the peace.

One of the most famous of these women was the lady-in-waiting Wang Zhaojun who was married to the Hun leader Huhanxie ("hoo-han-see-eh") in 33 B.C. A woman with a strong sense of duty toward her country, Wang Zhaojun volunteered to be the bride.

Wang Zhaojun had earlier been passed over during the selection of the emperor's consort. The story goes that the palace ladies bribed an artist to paint their portraits so that they appeared more beautiful than in real life, with the hope that the emperor might choose them. Only Wang Zhaojun refused to do this, and the artist made no effort on her portrait.

When she was brought into the court to appear before the emperor and meet Huhanxie, the emperor regretted he had not seen her earlier. (Picture shows statue of Wang Zhaojun.)

With jealousy an acceptable reason for getting rid of a wife, husbands could take concubines and blackmail their wives into silence. While these new codes were an improvement over earlier practices, women still remained highly vulnerable to their husband's whims, for they were without legal rights and protection.

Early marriage The Han court encouraged its subjects to marry early and have many children. Emperor Hui Di (195–188 B.C.) decreed that women over 15 who remained single would be subject to a poll tax five times the normal, while fathers would be excused from corvee labor (forced labor performed for the government) for the first two years of their children's lives. Later, mothers were exempted from taxes for three years after the births of their children, and fathers for one year. Pregnant women were given approximately 200 pounds of grain.

Promotions were given to officials who could report an increase in the population in their region. The government took care of all abandoned children.

Buddha image at the famous Longmen Grottoes in Luoyang, an ancient capital. This Buddha image is said to bear the features of the Tang empress, Wu Zetian.

Advent of Buddhism

After the collapse of the Han dynasty in A.D. 220, China was again divided, and no one leader was able to hold power for long. The years from A.D. 220 to 559 were turbulent years, with ambitious men, some of them chieftains of bordering tribes, seeking to conquer and rule China.

During this period Buddhism began to have an influence in China, having been introduced during the Han dynasty. The Buddhist sutras teach that both men and women can reach nirvana—that is, a state of oblivion after attaining high spirituality and wisdom.

In China one of the Buddhist deities took the form of a woman. This was Guan Yin or the Goddess of Mercy. Buddhist nuns had their heads shaved,

like the monks, and wore the same dress as monks. Buddhism in China accorded equality to men and women.

The Buddhists, in order to survive in China, had to consolidate their position. They did this by working closely with any faction of scholars that was in power in the bureaucracy. Gradually the Chinese Buddhists came to accept the Confucian codes of conduct that accorded unequal status to women. Later there were Buddhists who wrote false sutras to include ideas that men were superior to women and that giving birth was polluting to the earth.

Tang dynasty (618–907)

The short-lived Sui dynasty (A.D. 581–618) reunited China, but collapsed because of the misrule of the second emperor. Li Shimin, known in history as Emperor Tai Zong, founded the Tang dynasty, which became one of the greatest in Chinese cultural history. The dynasty flourished and was consolidated by Empress Wu, the wife of Li Shimin's son, Gao Zong. In turn, her grandson, Ming Huang, gave the empire half a century of peace during which the greatest Chinese poets and artists received his patronage.

The government machinery under the Tang rulers was highly organized and efficient. The Tang period was one of the great creative epochs of Chinese civilization. This was a period of the development of refined culture and a period of innovation and experimentation. It was a time too when many foreigners—Arabs, Persians, Jews—came to live in the capital Changan (present-day Xian) and other cities. Their cultures, philosophies, and religions enriched Chinese society.

It was during the reign of Empress Wu Zetian that religious art became more human and feminine. The feminization of the Bodhisattvas began, and it was from the 7th century that the Bodhisattva Avalokitesvara, known in China as Guan Yin, the Goddess of Mercy, the Hearer of the World's Cries, was given female form. (A Bodhisattva is one who has achieved great moral and spiritual wisdom but rejects nirvana in order to help the suffering.)

Traditional Confucianism remained the doctrine upon which the education system was based. Only men well versed in Confucian studies and who passed the imperial examinations could enter the government. Confucian ethics gave the government its moral authority and were an integral part of social thought.

Tang society As during the Han dynasty, marriages were arranged by parents. Early marriages were also encouraged. In A.D. 627 men were required to marry at 20 and women at 15; in 716 men married at 15 and women at 13. With such early marriages when both parties were still growing up and the male was still studying, it was very easy for the wife to become a semi-servant of the family, having no really close relationship with her husband. As a result many men cultivated male friendships and had love affairs with courtesans.

During this period educated women had more opportunity to reveal their talents and their works of poetry and prose survive to this day. For women, society was still very oppressive, and what happiness women had was marred by tears, as shown by the many literary works telling of their loves and misfortunes.

Mural showing Tang court women. During the Tang period women had more opportunity to express themselves in literature.

The Tang book *Women's Ethics* stated that when a woman walked, she was not to turn her head. She was to speak without opening her mouth too widely. She must never laugh too loudly. She was to sit without moving her knees, stand without swaying her skirts, and to show happiness and anger with restraint.

Women and the law Life for the majority of women was firmly in the hands of men. The famous law of the Tang dynasty, which defined in detail rules and regulations on marriage, ensured that this was the case.

According to the law, when a couple became engaged, the families had to have a written agreement. Once the woman had signed this agreement, she was not allowed to go back on her word. If she did, she would be flogged 60 times. If there was no written agreement and the woman had accepted betrothal gifts but later refused to marry, she would receive the same punishment. If the woman broke her word and became engaged to another man, she received 100 strokes. If she married another man, she would be imprisoned for a year and a half.

The law gave the right to arrange marriages to parents, elder brothers, and senior relatives. Parents had the right to force their widowed daughters to remarry. When the parents died, neither sons nor daughters could marry during the mourning period.

Both men and women were punished with one year's imprisonment if they committed bigamy. If a woman left her husband and married another, she would be jailed for two years as it was stipulated that a woman should never desert her husband. The seven grounds for divorce, set down during the Han dynasty, were followed.

Under rules governing family relations, if the wife beat her husband, she would be imprisoned for a year and a half, but wife-beating was not punishable. If the wife injured her husband, she would be jailed four and a half years. The wife would be hanged if she beat her husband's parents or injured them. If the parents-in-law killed the daughter-in-law, they would be jailed for only three years.

The Tang laws also required a written agreement if a man took a concubine. The law stated that if a man was attracted to his maid and she bore him a child, she should be taken as a concubine. And if the wife reached age 50 and still bore no children, she could be deserted and the concubine could become the wife. In the Tang dynasty many men had concubines they loved. Husband and wife relations were based on family status, wealth, and ethical principles, whereas concubines, whose status was low, had more intimate relations with the husband.

An unmarried daughter had the right to inherit family property even if she had brothers. But her share was half that of her brothers.

Empress Wu Zetian

Empress Wu Zetian is the only woman to have ruled from the imperial throne of China and commanded supreme power in both fact and name. For 50 years she proved herself an able ruler.

She ruled like a great Chinese emperor—with vision, and sometimes justice; she knew how to use men, and when to be drastic and ruthless. She paid attention to agriculture and under her rule China prospered. However, she remains one of the most maligned figures in Chinese history primarily because of the fact that she was a woman.

She was beautiful and talented, entering the palace at the age of 13 as a *guiren*, or concubine of the fifth rank. Her story is a fascinating one of intense court intrigue, murder, injustice, and twists of fate. But above all she was a wise ruler; the peace and unity she established in China paved the way for the great Tang era of cultural and artistic development.

Song dynasty (960–1279)

According to the census of A.D. 754, the population of China was over 52 million. Ten years later, after a bloody rebellion brought about the collapse of the Tang dynasty, the population had dropped to nearly 17 million. The fall of the Tang dynasty was followed by 53 years of partition and anarchy.

The Song dynasty (960–1279) marked the reunion of a nation that was weary of war.

The Song period represents one of the greatest ages of Chinese culture. The empire was at peace and the economy prospered. The five Song emperors were the most tolerant, humane, artistic, and intellectual rulers China had ever known. Poetry, history, and art flourished, leaving as legacy the exquisite Song *ci* ("tse," poetry written to a tune) and Song paintings the quality of which has never been equalled. China's greatest woman poet, Li Qingzhao ("lee ching-jhah-oo"), lived during this period.

Opposite: Li Qingzhao. Although her marriage was arranged, she and her husband fell in love. Together they wrote a book on his hobby, which was the collecting of ancient inscriptions.

From a strolling peddler
I bought a branch of spring blossoms
Whose rosy cheeks
Are loaded with tears of dew drops.
Lest my love should say,
Your face is less fair than the flowers,
I stuck them aslant in my cloud-like tresses
So that he could compare.

—*Li Qingzhao*

It was in philosophy that perhaps the contribution of the Song dynasty was greatest, influencing greatly the later centuries of Chinese civilization. Two schools of thought arose, the conservatives and the reformers. The ideology of the conservatives, that of rigid Confucianism, finally triumphed. However, it was much later, during the Ming and Qing dynasties, that the ideas expounded were put into practice.

The peace and prosperity of the Song dynasty also led to a rapid population increase. On the eve of the Mongolian invasions in A.D. 1124, a census gave the population as 100 million.

Song women New ideas of the Song period did not improve women's lot. It was during this period that the cruel practice of foot-binding began.

The rules of marriage were rigid. They stated that the duties of a wife were only to have children, care for parents-in-law, and do household chores. If a man was divorced or widowed, he was permitted one concubine if he was over 40 and had no son. He was not allowed to make the concubine his wife or take another wife. Concubines had no status in the family at all.

There were also few divorces during the Song dynasty. Divorce was considered indecent and thought to bring bad luck. However, when a man was dissatisfied with his wife, he could mistreat her as he liked. And the "seven reasons for divorcing a wife" were still officially considered justifiable.

Nevertheless, not all these excessive rules were adhered to, and common sense, decency and humanity prevailed. Among the educated, daughters-in-law who were widowed young were assisted in their remarriage. There were parents who taught their daughters to read and write.

China's greatest woman poet, Li Qingzhao, who lived toward the end of the Song dynasty, was educated by her parents.

The poetry she wrote was mainly of love and nature, and how she pined for her husband when he left home on official business. Her exquisite descriptions of happiness and sadness, and of the beauty of nature, remain fresh to this day.

Child brides

The custom of child brides began during the Song dynasty. Prior to this there were "womb betrothals." That is, before a child was born, the parents would arrange its marriage with another family.

During the Song dynasty, however, the custom of taking child brides became prevalent. Girls from poor families were sold into families with sons. The families who bought the child brides were not necessarily much richer themselves. The girls would be 12 or 13 and their husband-to-be perhaps three or four or even a baby of six months. The girls would be used as a slave by the family and often abused. When the boys grew up, they married the girls and this saved the family money as they were able to avoid a huge wedding and the customary gifts.

An upper-class Beijing woman having her hair dressed. During the Qing period women's chastity was highly valued and when a husband died it was virtually impossible for the woman to remarry.

Qing dynasty (1644–1911)

After the Song dynasty, China was ruled by the Mongols who established the Yuan dynasty (1206–1368). Mongolian rule was followed by the Ming dynasty (1368–1644), during which Confucianism again became the dominant social force. The Ming dynasty was overthrown by a peasant revolt and in 1644 China once again came under foreign rule. The Manchus, a group of people from Manchuria to the northeast of Ming China, established the Qing dynasty.

The Manchus adopted Chinese customs and culture, and they accepted and protected the most rigid Confucian traditions.

Rules restricting women were even more extreme. Laws against widows and rebellious women were severe. If a wife tried to run away, she would be flogged 100 times. A woman who dared to remarry would be hanged. The law required that all marriages be arranged. Those who did not obey were punished.

The head of the family not only arranged his children's marriages but also his servants' marriages. More often than not, for his own convenience, the head of the family would not allow the maids to marry. A housemaid could be married at 30 or 40, and that was considered good enough. Most of them remained single all their lives.

During the Ming and Qing dynasties learning began to be seen as injurous to the virtue of women. It was thought that without learning women would be virtuous. More rigid attitudes led to the idea that women would be considered loose if they were literate. Writing poetry was considered proof of promiscuity, a trick played by frivolous women.

Women's chastity Women's chastity was considered all important. During the Ming and Qing dynasties this idea was carried to an extreme. The author of the *History of Ming* wrote that only 308 women were worthy of special praise for being chaste and virtuous. During the Qing dynasty the numbers of chaste women were supposed to have increased greatly and temples in their memory were scattered everywhere.

It was believed a woman's body

Empress Dowager Ci Xi

Empress Dowager Ci Xi (1835–1908) was born Orchid Yehonala to a noble Manchu family. By the age of 16 when she entered the palace as a concubine of the fifth rank, she had mastered the classics in both Chinese and Manchu and had learned to paint skilfully and write calligraphy. She was highly intelligent, capable, and ambitious. It was said she had a voice of velvet.

In 1855 Emperor Hsienfeng raised her to a higher rank. The emperor was young, dissolute, incapable, and weary of the crises that were facing the empire. He was therefore grateful for her passion for knowledge and politics and allowed her to help him manage state affairs. Thus, at an early stage, she entered the center of power.

In 1856 she gave birth to the emperor's only son, and in 1861 the emperor died. She became the empress dowager and was given the title Ci Xi. As her son was only six, she acted as regent. Her son died in 1873, and Ci Xi picked another minor for the throne—her nephew, who was known as Emperor Guang Xu—and again acted as regent.

Ci Xi lived at a time when Western imperialists were fast encroaching into other lands, looking for markets and raw materials. Educated only in the Chinese classics, she was profoundly ignorant of the West, of its histories and cultures, and of the industrial revolution. Consequently she was incapable of dealing with foreign intervention and aggression. Corruption was rife under Manchu rule, and as a result there were rebellions, the most devastating being the Taiping Rebellion from 1851–1864 (see page 28). At the same time the Manchus were forced to sign unequal treaties with Western powers, ceding ports and parts of the country to foreign control. Japan defeated China in battle in 1894 and the Manchus were again forced to sign a treaty in Japan's favor. China was weak and powerless in the face of imperialist aggression. Anti-Manchu feeling was high as the Chinese blamed the Manchus for China's ills. The Reform Movement in 1898, supported by the young Emperor Guang Xu, advocated constitutional monarchy. The movement ended in a bloodbath and the usurpation of power by Ci Xi. After this, she began to introduce a few reforms, but it was already too late.

There was a prophecy among the Manchus that one day a woman would rule over them and bring the dynasty to an end. When Ci Xi was dying, her last words were: "Never again allow a woman to hold supreme power in the state."

should not be seen by a man. Some women died of illness rather than allow a male doctor to examine them.

Wives and concubines were supposed to kill themselves or be killed after the death of the husband. Wives and concubines were supposed to kill themselves before the husbands went to war, so the men could leave home free from worry. When a woman's fiancee died, she had to marry a wooden tablet representing the dead man, even if she had never seen him before, and she had to remain single all her life, living with the dead man's family as no more than a servant.

The Taiping Rebellion

The last century of Qing rule saw the coming of the Europeans, who bought Chinese goods such as tea, silk, and porcelain. To balance the trade the British started selling opium to the Chinese. The Qing government's efforts to ban its sale led to a series of wars known as the Opium Wars, which the Chinese lost. The Chinese had to sign an unequal treaty with the British in 1842 in which ports were opened, land was ceded, and Hong Kong became a British colony. Soon other European nations were forcing the Qing government to sign similar treaties.

As a result of Western penetration into the country, Western influence began to spread throughout China. At the same time, the wars and unequal treaties drained the national coffers leading to high taxes and general hardship. The Qing government was also increasingly corrupt. The result was a peasant uprising in 1851, known as the Taiping Rebellion. Taiping means "great peace," reflecting the hope of the rebels to bring peace to the nation.

The uprising began in southern China and spread across half the country. It lasted 13 years.

The rebels' attitude toward women was revolutionary, and women played an important role in the rebellion. Its program gave women equal rights to land. In its political program, women were allowed to take imperial examinations, and they could be elected as officials and join the army. The regime also abolished arranged marriages and strictly forbade prostitution, slave trading, and foot-binding.

Although the rebellion failed, it sowed the seeds for future nationalism and continuing revolution. In the 1930s, young girls were listening eagerly to their grandmother's tales of how the Taiping women unbound their feet, were independent, and fought alongside men. The Taipings became an inspiration for future revolutionaries.

The Republic of China

Qing rule, weakened by corruption and Western imperialism, collapsed in 1911 following an army uprising in Wuhan, an important city in central China.

The Nationalists (Kuomintang), led by Sun Yat-sen, came into power, with Sun as president. However, Sun's power base was weak, and to avoid bloodshed, he stepped down in favor of Yuan Shihkai, a warlord.

After the death of Yuan in 1916, China was nominally ruled by a government in Beijing, but in fact, power was in the hands of regional warlords. It was not until the 1920s that the Nationalists, under the leadership of Chiang Kaishek, were able to achieve some unification.

The May 4th movement In 1919, after World War I, the Treaty of Versailles awarded Japan former German colonies in China. In protest, Beijing students held a demonstration on May 4, 1919, demanding that the Chinese government reject the treaty. Young women students took part in the demonstration, which quickly grew into a nationwide movement.

Under public pressure, the government refused to sign the treaty.

But the May 4th movement became more than a political one, and its influences were felt up to and beyond 1949. Before the student demonstrations intellectuals were already questioning old traditions and developing ideas for reform. The outburst served to spread the ideas and led to greater ferment.

During this period, the feminist movement became very active. Later a new generation of women writers such as Ding Ling and Bing Xin gained prominence, some with ideas on feminism that cut boldly across tradition.

Sun Yat-sen, the father of modern China. Because his power base was weak, there was no strong Chinese leader who could pull the Chinese together. After the fall of the Qing dynasty, the country fell into anarchy and civil war.

Ding Ling, feminist writer

The May 4th movement gave rise to a new generation of women writers in the 1920s and 1930s. Most of their writings explored the themes of love, emotions, and sexual relationships, and were closely related to their own lives and experiences. The writing was limited in scope.

Writing at this time was an expression of personal consciousness rather than a conscious women's literary movement. Ding Ling (1904–1982) was a writer who emerged during this time. As a young woman, she wrote Western-style feminist literature. For that, she was derided by Chinese society. Her son was born in 1930, but the child's father was executed by the Nationalists soon after. Later she escaped to the Communist base in Yanan.

Ding Ling wrote many short stories and novels. In China these have largely become famous as a result of the criticisms directed against them. *Miss Sophie's Diary* was one of the main targets.

An open and direct person who acted on what she believed to be right, Ding Ling offended many, particularly Chinese men.

In 1942 she wrote *Thoughts on March 8th*, defining what being a woman should mean in a revolutionary world. This essay offended the male Communist hierarchy and she was criticized for it. In 1957 she was again criticized as a rightist and remained for the rest of her life a "disgraced" writer. She was rehabilitated after the Cultural Revolution.

To liberate feet

During the Song dynasty in the 12th century a new regulation was given to restrict the movements of women. A strip of wood was fixed onto the soles of their shoes so that every step they took was heard. Soon women were made to bind their feet as this "restrained their bodies," "ensured that they walked properly," and "softened their dispositions."

Foot-binding was a means of keeping women well under the thumb of men. A woman was crippled and imprisoned in her own house. By the end of the Song dynasty, it was unnatural to have unbound feet, and women who did not bind their feet could not find a good match.

The torture began when the girl was five or six years old. The binding was a strip of cloth about two inches wide and nine feet long. All five toes were turned under and bound beneath the arch of the foot. The long binding was then wrapped around the foot from the arch to the instep and then to the heel, which was made to touch the toes, the whole foot being restrained in a tiny grotesque arch. The binding was securely sewn on. The standard size of a bound foot was three inches long.

The daughters of peasants did not have their feet bound from childhood because they had to work in the house and in the fields. Very often country girls only applied the bindings for their marriage or when they entered a city or attended a temple fair. On returning home they would remove them. In southern China, in Guangdong and Guangxi provinces, where women traditionally worked in the fields, most women had unbound feet.

It was men who first spoke out against this cruel practice. In the early 1820s during the Qing Dynasty, Li Ruzhen wrote a satirical novel called *Jin Hua Yuan*, in which he had men take the place of women and described a man's suffering when his feet were bound. In the 1870's Western missionaries in China began working against foot-binding.

But it was not until 1901 that an imperial edict prohibited the practice of foot-binding.

At the same time, Western ideas of civil rights and sexual equality began to penetrate Chinese society, leading to a women's movement. By then many educated women had begun to take part in the unbound feet movement.

As the revolutionary movement to overthrow the Qing dynasty developed, foot-binding was no longer the central issue for women's liberation. Yet it played an important part in the history of the Chinese women's liberation movement because it began the attack on the traditional ideas of sexual discrimination. Most important, the prohibition of foot-binding began to free women physically. They began to go to school and to study abroad. Progressive women now made their first efforts to promote the idea of total liberation of their sex.

The Revolution of 1911 legally put an end to foot-binding. However, it took another 38 years before the custom was completely eliminated.

Women's movements

The Nationalists and Communists had their separate women's movement.

The Communist women's movement emphasized equality of the sexes and freedom to choose a marriage partner. In practice, women were given the right to work and fight alongside men. The Communist women's movement appealed to many women who had suffered under the system of arranged marriages and who were unable to obtain an education or work.

The Nationalist government issued an order stating that women had the right to choose their husbands, to divorce, and to inherit property as well as to equal pay for equal work, but this was hardly enforced. Instead the Nationalists established a New Life Movement that emphasized a woman's duty to stay at home and care for her husband and children. It supported legislation that gave a husband the right to demand that his wife be dismissed from her job if it caused strife in their household.

The Nationalist approach to the women's movement was one of upholding tradition coupled with gradual reform. The Communists stressed revolution and equality of the sexes.

The Chinese Communist Party The Chinese Communist Party was formed in 1921 by young intellectuals, some of whom had been student leaders in the May 4th movement.

In 1924 the Nationalists and Communists formed a United Front to unify China. However, this was broken by the Nationalists in 1927, and the Communists were forced underground.

Continued attacks by the Nationalists finally forced the Communists to abandon their bases in the southeast. Between 1934 and 1935, 130,000 Communist soldiers marched thousands of miles on foot to start a new base in northwest China. A number of women took part in the Long March, as it is known.

Later, during the war of resistance against the Japanese who invaded China in 1937, thousands of young women went to the Communist bases in the northwest. There many attended schools and the university. Many also took part in production to help the war effort, and others received medical training and nursed the sick and wounded.

Women workers at the Communist base in Yanan, wearing overalls that bear the Communist star. Patriotic women left their homes to join the Communists when Japan invaded central and south China in 1937.

The Marriage Law

One of the most important laws passed after the establishment of the People's Republic of China was the Marriage Law of 1950. This law gave women the right to choose their own husbands. It also gave women the right to file for divorce, to inherit property, to have equal status in the home and the workplace, and to use their own surnames. The Marriage Law gave protection to women and children for the first time in China's history.

Furthermore, the government set up a program to implement the law. Thousands of women from the All-China Women's Federation (see Chapter 6) and the justice department traveled the country telling people what the Marriage Law meant.

Many women began to apply for divorce. Men who had left their villages to join the revolution also divorced the wives they had left behind. This angered many people, and in some places the Marriage Law was dubbed the "Divorce Law."

Women's rights workers were seen by the government as being too rash and as using the Marriage Law to oppress men. In 1953, a directive was issued in which the women's federation was told to work more slowly.

The Marriage Law was revised in 1980. Amendments were made changing the legal marriageable age for a man from 20 to 22 and for a woman from 18 to 20. A breakdown in mutual affection was recognized as a reason for divorce, whereas in the earlier law, divorce on this basis was not possible.

People's Republic of China

When the Japanese army invaded China proper in 1937, another United Front between the Communists and Nationalists was formed. Together they defeated the Japanese, but afterward the country fell again into civil war. In 1949 the Communists defeated the Nationalists, whose government had become corrupt and weak, and established the People's Republic of China.

The first constitution of the People's Republic of China, passed in 1951, stipulated equality of the sexes. Chinese society came to accept the social as well as the economic need for women to work. Women activists also took part in the political movements of the time, such as land reform, and later in the many political movements the Communists organized.

The great leap forward In 1958 Communist leader Mao Zedong launched the campaign known as the Great Leap Forward. This was to increase economic output and encourage technical innovation.

The People's Communes were formed throughout the countryside, and they took over government at the district level. They directed what was to be produced and assigned jobs to people. During this time, women, whether they wanted to or not, were pressured to work outside the home.

The Cultural Revolution The programs of the Great Leap Forward failed, and Mao was forced to take a back seat by some party members. To regain control, he launched the Cultural Revolution to purge those who opposed him.

Claiming that the country was becoming capitalist, he called on the people to attack old ideas, old culture, old habits, and old customs. Young people were mobilized to bring back the "real spirit of revolution." These young people formed the Red Guards, who went around the country terrorizing intellectuals and destroying historical relics, books, and temples.

Urban intellectuals and young people were sent to the countryside to work on the land and learn "revolutionary values" from the peasants. Family life was disrupted, and mothers were forced to leave their children behind when they went to the countryside to work.

The Cultural Revolution caused chaos to the country and brought its economy to the brink of ruin. It ended in 1976, but its effects are still felt today.

Beyond revolution After the Cultural Revolution, the government began the enormous task of bringing the country back to normal. Under the leadership of Deng Xiaoping, economic reforms began.

Over the past decade, changes in Chinese society have been great. The government has set up special economic

Factory worker. In the 1950's women were pressured to work outside the home.

zones along the coast, where joint ventures with foreign investors are encouraged. Workers in the zones are paid according to their skills and productivity, rather than receiving low, uniform wages as was the norm for so long.

In general, the reforms have brought about a measure of prosperity, but there are problems. In particular, women are finding that some old ideas have resurfaced. For example, discrimination against women at the workplace has increased as the government has given managers a freer hand in hiring and firing.

On the other hand, some women are finding that the freer economic climate has led to opportunities to develop themselves to the fullest.

chapter three

Women in Society

The face of China has changed dramatically over the past 40 years. Provinces and cities throughout the entire country have been linked by road, rail and air transportation. Industry and commerce, both domestic and overseas, have expanded rapidly while education, the arts, and science have also developed. In all these fields as well as in defense, women have played an important and indispensible role.

Beginning in the 1950s, education and employment opportunities began to expand for women.

There are around 60 million women of working age (16–54) in Chinese cities and townships. Of these, 51 million are employed in some form of production. In the vast rural areas of China there are more than 180 million women of working age. They represent half of the agricultural working population and till the fields, raise poultry and pigs, herd sheep and cattle, and work their private plots. Still, to a great degree, they live a life of semi-poverty.

Opposite and right: Worker at metalworks and a city professional. Whether working in heavy industry or commerce, the women of China have shown that they can hold their own. Their achievements have been outstanding.

Nonetheless, the achievements of Chinese women in their various fields have been outstanding. They have contributed greatly to China's development and success. Like women all over the world, Chinese women have shown that once given the chance, they are able to hold their own. This is despite the fact that in most if not all fields of work, men are still the dominant force.

China's economic reforms

China's economic reforms began in 1979 in the countryside and by 1984 had spread to the cities.

In the rural areas In the countryside the most significant thing that occurred was the dismantling of the People's Communes. For 20 years the People's Communes had been in charge of both government administration and agricultural production. Under the reforms, the local prefectural government was reestablished, and instead of receiving orders from the government on what to produce, villagers could decide for themselves what they and the market wanted. Families were given land to manage for themselves under a contract system.

In 1985, farmers were not required to sell all their produce to the state. Instead they sold fixed amounts of their produce to the state at state-fixed prices. They were permitted to sell freely the remaining produce at market prices. This new system increased the efficiency of agricultural production.

The peasants prospered. However, new problems have arisen as increased efficiency has reduced the need for agricultural workers. Many farmers have become migrant workers traveling around China looking for work. Some farmers have been absorbed into rural industry. Others who have business

Prejudice and production

Yunnan province is the home of many ethnic groups. In the past, the anti-illiteracy campaign drew very few ethnic women. Women were expected to remain at home. Attending meetings and learning anything new were men's business.

However, following the rural economic reforms, the land was divided up and contracted to individual farmers. Men went off to the townships to work and women were left on the farm to cope as best they could. Women began attending night schools or Women's Homes as they are called, where simple improvements in farming techniques are taught.

After attending a training course just after the reforms began, Xiong Huiying, of the Wa nationality, began experimenting on her farm, using manure, other kinds of fertilizers, and weed killers. These bold steps threw her relatives and elders into a rage. They accused her of breaking down the conventions of the clan. In the face of this pressure, Huiying realized that explanations would be useless and decided to convince them with facts. She persisted through to the autumn harvest when the yield on her land was three times the usual amount produced by traditional farming methods.

Almost overnight, Xiong became famous. Not only her fellow villagers, but people from neighboring villages came to seek her advice. Today she is an agricultural instructor.

acumen have developed the resources at their disposal and breed poultry and fish or grow flowers and fruit for city markets. Many of these entrepreneurs are women with little education.

Small town and rural enterprises

There are 15 million small town and rural enterprises across the country that employ 90 million rural residents, 35 million of whom are women. Some are run by the local Communist Party officials, others are run privately or as cooperatives. Their development is important in that rural people do not have to leave their homes although they have to stop farming. They produce a huge variety of goods such as electric fans, spare parts for electric fans and bicycles, textiles, buttons, door handles, knitwear, and furniture. In these small-scale industries, many women have demonstrated their talent for management and sales.

Specialized households

In other parts of rural China, specialized households have emerged where people pool their labor and enterprise to produce either cash crops or other products. Women head 35% to 40% of these households. One such woman is Zhang Guiru, who runs a chicken farm in Huairou county north of Beijing. She had only three years in primary school before dropping out to help the family in the fields. In

1983 she and her husband built a new house, which left them in debt.

Guiru thought perhaps she could help the family get out of debt if she raised chickens. This had never been done in the village before. Every household had chickens, but these were sold for daily necessities such as cooking oil, salt, and other goods. Nonetheless, she decided to try, and obtained a loan from the township credit cooperative with which she purchased 500 chickens. She spent hours studying books on poultry raising, and would even walk 20 miles to the county's chicken farm to seek advice.

Guiru's painstaking work paid off and in the first year she not only settled the entire family debt but also saved some money. Now she and her husband run a poultry farm with 12,000 chickens.

Harvest time. With economic reforms, people now work on their own land instead of on a large commune. They are also allowed to sell excess produce in the free markets. As a result, farming has become more efficient and production has risen.

In the cities In 1984 the focus of economic reform shifted to the cities. There the majority of enterprises were owned and run by the state as many still are today. These enterprises not only dealt in production but also looked after the welfare of the workers from cradle to grave. They had housing estates, elementary and high schools, and even part-time universities. There were medical clinics, hospitals, shops, and so on. Many of these enterprises ran at a loss and were heavily subsidized by the state. Because everything was provided for regardless of how the workers performed, most of the workers did not work hard and both productivity and quality of the goods suffered. The reforms aimed to change this situation.

The government began to allow the development of collective and individual enterprises as well as joint ventures between Chinese and foreign firms. Over the past seven years, there has been substantial development in these types of enterprise. This has resulted in the growth of a new type of work force. The collectively owned, individual and joint-venture enterprises have to account for their own profits or losses and cannot rely on any government assistance. This demands a

Woman go home

The Anshan Steel Company is one of China's oldest and biggest steel plants. It has a work force of over 20,000 with many women workers. Like all Chinese state enterprises, it was over-staffed. In 1985 Japanese management experts were called in. After investigation they suggested giving an examination all workers would be required to pass, doubling the wages of the workers who remained so they could support a family, and sending women workers home to look after their husbands and families properly to leave the male workers free to cope with production problems. The All-China Women's Federation opposed this and wrote a report to the Politbureau saying that such a proposition threatened women's right to work. The Politbureau upheld the Federation's position and the Japanese proposal was never implemented.

In 1990, the clothing factory of the Anshan Steel Company began to implement part of the Japanese proposal. This factory makes the work clothes for the steel workers and employs 366 women. It was operating at a loss and elected a 32-year-old director, Hu Youming. Seeing that the average age of women workers was 26, the new director calculated that some 200 of them would have babies in the coming three years. He set up a system allowing women to sign a contract with the factory defining output, quality, and schedules on working at home for the same regular wage and bonuses.

However, only 66 women have signed up for the work-at-home plan. Most are wary and think this might be a way of getting rid of them.

motivated and productive work force that is rewarded according to ability and productivity. This motivational change has resulted in increased industrial output.

Reaching for the top In industry and commerce there are women who, although not well educated, have a natural talent for business and administration, and who have made their mark through persistence and hard work.

In 1953 when she was 15, Yang Jinghua began working in the supply and marketing cooperative of Hucun Village in Shanxi province. (Situated in northwestern China, Shanxi province is one of the poorer provinces where male patriarchal biases are strong and opportunities for women in rural areas few and far between.)

The co-op sold groceries, clothing, and daily necessities. Through years of hard work, Yang became head of the cooperative and turned it into a rural comprehensive center that not only produced goods but sold them as well.

She organized the villagers to run a pig farm, a bee farm, and a sheep farm, and converted the local brewery to produce daily necessities like vinegar and bean paste for the farmers. It also processed meat and other provisions, baked cakes, and produced clothing, shoes, and hats.

In 1975 Yang Jinghua was transferred to Yuci ("yoo-tse") county and was

appointed deputy head of the county in charge of finance and trade. This county was very poor and relied mainly on relief grants from the province. Yang Jinghua saw the county's potential and decided to set up a vinegar factory. The vinegar was later cited as an excellent product by the Ministry of Commerce and sold well nationwide. The county's canning factory later was expanded to include meat as well as fruit and soft drinks.

These successes not only erased the county's financial deficit but left it with a profit. Yang Jinghua is now deputy mayor of Yuci city.

Textile worker. While economic reforms have created new opportunities for women, they have also brought about problems. Managers who are now free to hire and fire tend to hire women last and fire them first.

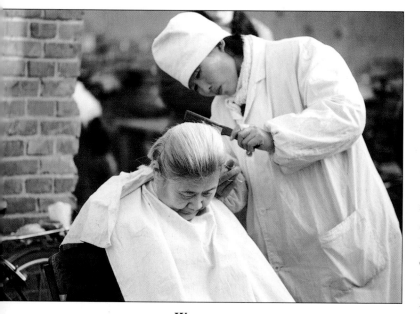

Above and opposite: Sidewalk hairdresser and vendor. Many enterprising women have gone into business for themselves, first starting a small sidewalk stall, then acquiring a store.

hotel's administration, and since then the hotel has doubled its profits each year.

In 1990 Liu decided to renovate the hotel. She did this by working on one room at a time so the hotel could maintain 95% of its business. As a result of her detailed planning, the hotel saved about $180,000.

Liu Aizhi has a sense of the new, and after tasting a herbal meal in Shanghai, she contacted the Chinese Medicinal Institute. With their cooperation the hotel created several herbal dishes. They were a great success, particularly with guests from Japan and Southeast Asia.

There are many other women managers who have learned how to work in the new conditions of the joint ventures, which require strict employee discipline. They have learned to handle diplomatically countless sensitive issues such as recruiting or dismissing workers, increasing or decreasing workers' salaries, and appointing or removing staff from top posts.

All of these are new to the Chinese, as enterprises in China have never been managed in Western style.

Individual employment Of 21 million self-employed people, one-third or 5 million are women. To become self-employed, apart from obtaining a license for a fee stipulated by the government,

Women managers in joint ventures
Joint-venture enterprises with Chinese and foreign capital only began in the 1980s. Since then more than 20,000 joint ventures have opened in China. A number of women managers have emerged in these companies.

Liu Aizhi was born in 1942 and began her career as a hotel assistant when she was a teenager. She has worked in all the areas of the hotel industry, which has given her a solid foundation in hotel management.

Since the beginning of 1988, Liu Aizhi has been general manager of the Lujiang Hotel, a joint venture with a Hong Kong-based company. This hotel is in Fujian province by the Xiamen seaside. As soon as she took her new position, Liu Aizhi reorganized the one must also have sufficient capital to purchase stock.

Some young people have begun at the bottom, first becoming street vendors selling food, clothing, and other goods, or renting a small room near home and setting up services such as hairdressing. After they have accumulated capital, they can then set up a store. The more successful have opened fashion boutiques, bookstores, tailoring shops, and other enterprises. Most, however, are street vendors selling articles from hardware to cigarettes, fruit and clothing to food.

These self-employed young people, especially the women, had to stand up to a great deal of social discrimination when they started out in the late 1970s and early 1980s. Many people, including their parents, were against their going into private business. Being a merchant or a small-time salesman has been at the low end of the Chinese social scale since ancient times. The Communists have also treated private business with suspicion. Even in the early 1980s people despised private self-employment and still considered government jobs the most prestigious.

However, by the 1990s this social attitude had fundamentally changed. The government does not have enough jobs for the tremendous number of young people in China—60% of the population is 45 and under—and

individual employment is an important means of solving the employment problem. Moreover, the majority of self-employed workers make more money than those in government, and this is increasing its appeal. However, self-employed workers have to work far longer hours, have few holidays, and have no security with regard to health, disability, and old age.

Wu Yi

Wu Yi is the deputy minister of the Ministry of Foreign Economic Relations and Trade. She graduated from the Petroleum College in 1962 and worked in Beijing's Yanshan Petrochemical Works for 20 years. There she rose from a lowly technician to general engineer to deputy manager of the corporation, and finally to its party secretary. This is the highest position of power in any government body in China. Beijing's Yanshan Petrochemical Corporation is the nation's fifth largest enterprise with an annual output of about $600 million.

In 1988 Wu Yi was elected deputy mayor of Beijing, responsible for industry and foreign trade. During the three years she was in charge of foreign trade, Beijing saw an increase in volume to the total of $1 billion. Wu Yi said, "I'm conscious of one fact: generally speaking, few men like to work under a female boss."

From the very beginning Wu earned a reputation for being strict. At the first meeting she chaired as deputy mayor, she began punctually. The meeting was attended by leaders of important corporations and enterprises. Several of them arrived late, and looking for empty seats, began freely greeting their acquaintances regardless of the fact that she was speaking.

Wu stopped the meeting and said, "I'm speaking. Do you always come late and speak to one another when someone is talking?" From then on, no one arrived late or talked during Wu Yi's meetings.

Women in politics

In China men play the dominant role in politics. The most powerful body of the government is the Politbureau of the Chinese Communist Party, which has no woman. Of 285 members of the Party's Central Committee there are only 22 women, a representation of 12%.

The National People's Congress, China's legislature, has 634 women deputies, representing only 21.3%.

There is one woman vice-premier out of six. There are 12 women deputy ministers.

In local government there is only one woman provincial governor, and 12 women are deputy provincial governors.

Education

The government has instituted a nine-year compulsory education system that was included in the 1982 constitution. It also passed the Compulsory Education Law on April 12, 1986. The government spends 13% of its budget on education, which is still insufficient to provide a universal nine-year education program for the enormous population. There are insufficient numbers of qualified teachers and too few school buildings and other equipment. Elementary education in China is neither free nor universal.

There are nearly 4 million women teachers, which is about 40% of the teaching ranks. Of these almost 2.5 million teach in elementary schools. The pay is low, and conditions are also poor in terms of housing and other facilities.

Teacher of a special rank Li Ruirong has earned herself the distinctive title "Teacher of a Special Rank" in her province. She has just retired after having taught the first grade for more than 30 years in Zhengzhou City.

Li Ruirong's methods of teaching differ a great deal from those of the majority of Chinese teachers. On their first school day she will make sure the children feel happy and at home. She will take them on walks around the school and explain the things they need to know.

In the classroom, she believes in

arousing the children's interest as she feels that this helps them to learn. She says, "I don't object to classroom rules, but I hate to let the children sit there for 40 minutes with their hands behind their backs just listening to the teacher." (This is the position in which students learn in Chinese elementary schools.)

"I want the children to think for themselves, develop their imagination, and consider the classroom as a place where they can obtain knowledge," she says.

Li Ruirong has devised methods in which her pupils learn through games, riddles, and rhymes.

Above: Class in progress. Women make up nearly half of the schoolteachers in China. More than half of them teach in elementary school.

Opposite: Women delegates to the National People's Congress. In politics, women are under-represented.

Science and technology

Above: Prof. Ni Yixin

Below: Jin Qingmin and her young assistants discussing their findings with a Dutch geologist, during the 1991 expedition to the Antartica.

According to official figures in 1990, China has 758,901 scientists and technicians, of whom 3,517 are women.

Professor Ni Yixin of Qinghua University is the first woman to hold a PhD. in engineering in China. She was given the title Honorary Scholar and Consultant by Iowa State University, the first time in its 100-year history the title has been given to an international exchange scholar. This was the result of the work she did on a research project on power systems. Her findings received high acclaim.

Professor Ni now engages in research and teaching.

Jin Qingmin ("jin ching-min"), who graduated from the Beijing Geological College in 1961, has been to the Antarctic three times. One of her teachers describes Jin as a natural geologist, both gifted and lucky. In 1986 she was the only one selected to go to the Antarctic from the staff at the Ministry of Geology and Mineral Resources. She joined China's Antarctic Expedition Team for a 77-day geological inspection. She was the only woman on the team, and some of the men complained that it was not convenient to have a woman along. They were also not too happy that an extra toilet had to be dug because of her.

In 1988 Jin Qingmin was also one of the members of the Sino-American South Pole Scientific Expedition Team to explore the highest peak—Vinson Massif—in Antarctica. They ventured far into the land and discovered a large iron deposit. In 1991 she went to Antarctica with the seventh South Pole Expedition Team of China as head of its geological inspection team. She led eight young researchers in their task to conduct geological surveys on the South Shetland Islands.

Within 17 days they had completed various geological survey maps covering 7.6 square miles and collected 993 geological samples, making new discoveries in hydrology and marine deposits. They returned to their research institute in Nanjing to continue their studies.

Medicine and health

There are 1.25 million women health workers, which is a little more than half of all the workers in this profession. China today provides free medicine and health care for 26.5 million people out of 1.1 billion inhabitants. To receive free medical care one must be on the state payroll, that is, work in a state organization or enterprise, or be a college student. This free medical care is primarily provided in the cities, counties, and towns. The rest of China has to pay for its medical care, and in the vast rural areas highly trained and experienced medical personnel are not easy to find.

China has trained a number of women doctors over the past 40 years. They work in all fields in varying conditions and are particularly prevalent in gynecology and pediatrics.

The majority of gynecologists and obstetricians are women; Chinese women are not accustomed to consulting male gynecologists.

There are 60,991 trained urban midwives. In the rural areas there are 320,000 women rural doctors. These women receive shorter training periods

A hospital nursery. In medicine, many women specialists are gynecologists or pediatricians.

than regular doctors. There are also 440,000 rural midwives who are trained in the townships or in county hospitals. The training of midwives and first aid workers in the rural areas has been continuing for many years and these individuals have become indispensible in delivering health care in the countryside. This is important because most hospitals are far from the country villages where the only transportation is by cart or bicycle. Because they live nearby, midwives can be called in at any time of day or night to deliver a baby.

Midwives are trained in basic Western medical practices, and also learn traditional Chinese medical practices such as the use of acupuncture to dislodge the placenta. Gynecology is an integral part of traditional Chinese medicine, much of which is simple, effective, and economic.

Women music lovers

Zheng Xiaoying ("jheng see-ao-ying"), China's first woman conductor, studied in Moscow 30 years ago. There, she would sit on the bank of the Moscow River with two other young Chinese women, and they would talk about founding their own orchestra.

Thirty years later, they did just that. In March 1990 the Women's Philharmonic Chamber Orchestra, or the Ai Yue Nu ("women music lovers"), was founded, with Xiaoying as conductor, art director, and announcer.

The Ai Yue Nu is an amateur society founded by a group of excellent women musicians who funded it themselves. These 18 women, some grandmothers, gave over 60 performances in Beijing in the first two years.

They also have held Chinese music concerts, developing their own style. Ai Yue Nu has rearranged Chinese traditional music for their chamber orchestra and boldly introduced Chinese musical instruments in concertos.

The chamber orchestra is proving very popular, even with young audiences.

Music

In music many women have shown great talent.

Most major cities in China have symphony orchestras and all have women members. The Central Philharmonic Orchestra has 119 members of whom 14 are women.

China's first woman orchestra conductor, Zheng Xiaoying, is senior conductor with the Central Opera Theater in Beijing. She was invited in 1988 to conduct *Madame Butterfly* at the Vaasa Opera Theatre in Finland.

In Western opera, soprano Hu Xiaoping, who won first prize at the Kodaly-Erkel International Singing Competition in Budapest in 1982, was originally a Shanghai textile worker. Liang Ning is a mezzo-soprano who graduated from the Beijing Central Conservatory of Music in 1983. She has won awards in Britain and Finland, including the first prize in the women's division of the Mirjam Helin International Singing Contest in Finland.

There are a number of women composers and women teachers of musical composition. Qu Xixian ("choo shee-shien") has composed many popular songs for children and choral pieces and the score for the film *Rickshaw Boy*.

In traditional Chinese music, one of the most brilliant virtuosos on the *er hu*, a Chinese two-stringed instrument, is Min Huifen. She has been playing since she was eight years old, having been taught by her father, a professor of traditional folk music at the Nanjing Normal University. Her playing has been acclaimed both at home and abroad.

Traditional opera

China is rich in traditional opera. There are many types and styles, the most well known of which is the Beijing opera.

The Cultural Revolution did much to destroy traditional Chinese opera, with its stories about emperors, ministers, generals, and beauties or legends that the Communists considered to be feudal, backward, and immoral. Thus a whole generation grew up never hearing or knowing of these operas. Since the Cultural Revolution, television has contributed to a further decline in the popularity of traditional opera. People prefer watching foreign programs to local traditional works.

Yue Opera, which belongs to

Shanghai and the neighboring Jiangsu and Zhejiang regions, has traditionally been sung by women. It has its own gentle lilting tunes and is sung in the Zhejiang dialect.

In 1947 a group of Yue opera singers who called themselves Ten Sisters formed an experimental theater and a Yue opera school. In old China an opera singer had very low social status, and these women singers were particularly vulnerable to sexual harassment by wealthy men.

After 1949, the 10 women received recognition as artists and continued to sing in operas, becoming household names in China. During the Cultural Revolution all 10 were hounded by the radicals, imprisoned, and humiliated. As a result one committed suicide and another suffered a stroke. Since the Cultural Revolution some have performed, but now they teach.

Yue opera artistes in costume. Yue opera is sung by women.

A film production in progress. Chinese women directors are beginning to make their mark on the film industry, while women actors have found fame at home and abroad.

Cinema

It is through the generation of young directors, most of whom graduated from the Beijing Film Academy in 1982, that Chinese films have won acclaim at recent international film festivals as well as from audiences worldwide. Many of these new filmmakers grew up during the Cultural Revolution, spending their youth in remote farms or grimy factories, and their films express their experience.

The film *Hibiscus Town*, set in the 1960s and 1970s, traces the tragic effects of the Cultural Revolution on the people of a small town. *Yellow Earth* subtly shows the disparity between the words and actions of a Communist when called upon to save a young girl from the tragic fate of an arranged marriage. Other films have come on the international scene recently, such as *Red Sorghum*, *Judou*, and *Raise the Red Lantern*, all of which reveal a subtle freshness in dealing with the reality of the complex fabric of Chinese society.

Huang Shuqin is one of the new generation directors. Born in 1940, she worked as an assistant director after the Cultural Revolution, and began to direct her own films in 1981. Her film, *Long*

Live the Youth, which depicts the lives of high school students in the 1960s, was controversial, and at first no film studio wanted to produce it.

Her other films, *Friends in Childhood* and *Actions Go Beyond Boundaries*, have all won awards. In 1987 her film *Ghosts and Human Beings*, which tells the story of a traditional opera singer Qiuyun who makes a success of her career at the cost of her own family and happiness, won her the most awards. It won the best scriptwriter award (Shuqin wrote her own script) at the 8th China Film Awards. It also won the Golden Bird Award for best picture at the Rio de Janeiro International Film–TV Festival in Brazil and the 8th Public Grand Prix of Feature Films at the French International Women's Film Festival. In 1990 Shuqin directed a 10-episode television series *Besieged City*. This was an adaptation of the famous novel by Qian Zhongshu about a group of young people in the 1930s and their life experiences. She won a best director award for this work.

Of China's 10 top-rated film stars in 1990, five were women. One of them is Yu Lan, who was born in northeastern China and is famous for her portrayals of working women and revolutionary women. Bai Yang, who was born in Beijing, started her film career at the age of 11. She became famous before 1949 after she played Li Sufen, a gentle

and faithful but tragic woman worker in the *River Flows East*. Xie Fang distinguished herself in 1958 by playing the role of Lin Daojin, a revolutionary woman intellectual in the 1930s in the film *Song of Youth*. Liu Xiaoqing won the 1980 Hundred Flowers Award for best supporting actress and both the 1987 and 1988 Hundred Flowers Award for best leading actress. Pan Hong is nicknamed "star of tragedy," as she mostly plays tragic figures. She has acted in such films as *A Bitter Smile, At Middle Age, Du Shi Niang, Well, The Bitter Cold Night*, and the *Last Aristocrat*. Pan Hong won the 1989 Hundred Flowers Award for best leading actress.

Pan Hong (second from right) one of the top 10 film stars in China, is known as the "star of tragedy."

Bai Shuxiang, one of the most talented ballet dancers to emerge during the 1950s, when ballet was newly-introduced in China. She is today the assistant director of the Central Ballet Troupe.

Ballet

This is a comparatively young art form in China, having been introduced to the country only in the 1940s. It was British-trained ballerina Dai Ailian who brought ballet to China, and in 1950, the Beijing Dance Company was formed, the first of its kind in the country. In 1959 the Central Ballet Troupe was established. It is still the most famous ballet company in China.

In the 1950s Soviet artists taught Russian classical ballet to a corps of dancers, teachers, choreographers, and directors. One of the most talented dancers at the time was Bai Shuxiang who now teaches. In the late 1950s and early 1960s the ballet was blended with Chinese stories and lavish dance dramas were staged.

The Cultural Revolution put a stop to all this and for many years there was no ballet and no dance dramas. After 1976 ballet schools were reestablished.

Ballet is now enjoying a revival, with the emphasis on creating local ballets.

At present Beijing and Shanghai have ballet schools. China has also invited well-known ballet artists from Australia, Britain, Canada, and the United States to perform and to coach Chinese dancers.

Ballerina Dai Ailian's teacher of the 1930s, British ballet master Anton Dolin, was invited to teach in 1983 at the age of 80.

Women in art

There are many outstanding women artists in China. Chinese women artists range from traditional Chinese painters to those who work in oils and water-colors, to designers of fabric and porcelains.

Yu Feng is one of China's noted women artists and art critics. She first studied painting at the Beijing Art Academy in 1930–33. She then went to the Fine Arts Department of Nanjing

An art class. There are many outstanding Chinese women artists, trained in the Western as well as Chinese art styles.

University where she studied Western art and painting.

In the 1950s and 1960s Yu Feng worked at the Beijing Artists' Association, and was mainly responsible for the organization of exhibitions at the Central Gallery of Art.

In 1982 she participated in the French Salon Exhibition where her painting "Awakening in Spring" was awarded a gold prize. She paints in both oils and watercolors.

Chang Shana was born in 1931. Her father was one of the first artists to study in France. Upon returning he went to the Dunhuang Caves in northwest China to study the ancient Tang dynasty Buddhist cave murals.

Chang Shana grew up in Dunhuang and has painted copies of the murals as well as developed her own style of ornamental art. Since the 1970s she has been the director of the Central Academy of Fine Arts.

Nie Ou was born in 1948 and during the Cultural Revolution went to work in a village in Shanxi province. After graduating from the Central Academy of Fine Arts, she remained as a member of the staff. Her speciality is ink brush painting depicting the lives of people in the rural north.

Many books by women writers have been translated into English, including Zhang Jie's *Love Must Not Be Forgotten*.

Women writers

Nineteen seventy-nine might be regarded as a turning point in the development of contemporary literature in China. The Cultural Revolution had been repudiated and the flow of literature in its wake told of the horrors, the woes and the injustices that occurred during that period. This trend, however, was soon stopped. Nonetheless it was the beginning of new ideas and approaches to literature. Women writers over the years had basically applied themselves to general themes. Most had never taken up women's problems as their main theme. However, there are now more women writers who are voicing women's issues in their work.

Zhang Jie, a Manchu, was the first woman novelist to deal with the issues of widespread bias against women. Her novel *Love Must Not Be Forgotten* (1979) struck a raw nerve in Chinese society and was tremendously popular with young people. In this novel she calls into question the old moral code that a woman must bow to her husband's wishes all her married life.

Another issue women writers are highlighting is the right of women to pursue their careers on the same basis as men and to be accorded the same personal dignity as men. They point out that enterprising women do not get the support they need from either their families or society. In her book *On the Same Horizon* (1982) Zhang Xinxin gives a frank portrayal of the heroine's inner suffering when she comes to realize she must make a choice between family and career. She suggests that the conflicting demands between the conventional expectation that women be "virtuous and able wives and good mothers" and the desire of women to make full use of their abilities in the workplace can only lead to deteriorating relations between husbands and wives and marital breakdown. The novel aroused much heated public discussion when it was released.

Divorce may provide a way out of the dilemma but as Zhang Jie shows in her short story *Ark* it is no escape from hardship. *Ark* chronicles the difficulties

A Chinese Winter's Tale

Yu Luojin has never been recognized in China by the authorities as a writer. Nonetheless her writing became well known in the early 1980s, particularly by people her own age. She belongs to what is called the "lost generation," the group that missed out on schooling during the Cultural Revolution.

Luojin has been noted for her bold narrative of the dark side of Chinese society, and for her persistent search for love and truth. She has tried to be honest about subjects such as love and sex, marriage and divorce in a culture where there has never been the freedom to be honest. She has been attacked by Communist Party authorities as a "fallen woman" and as a "handmaiden of the bourgeoisie." Life was made intolerable for her and she now lives abroad.

Her best known work is *A Chinese Winter's Tale,* which is an intensely personal account of a young woman's experiences during the Cultural Revolution. It tells the story of the author's marriage, her traumatic discovery of her own sexual ignorance, the repeated beatings she suffered at her husband's hands, and a love affair that seems first to offer a rebirth of feeling, but ultimately leads to an even more profound disenchantment.

The story is also a social document. Its harrowing account of the arrest, imprisonment, and execution of the author's brother, its vivid depiction of Red Guard violence, of political paranoia, and of daily life in a Chinese labor camp and in the backward countryside of the "Great Northern Wilderness," and its emotional honesty have made it one of the most widely read and controversial works of literature in contemporary China.

faced by three divorcees as they pursue their careers. Their struggle for dignity and recognition in a male-dominated society that considers divorced women somewhat tainted, pushes them to the brink of mental and physical exhaustion.

Chinese society is male-centered. The bias against women is perpetuated not only by men but also by some women themselves. Women have to put twice as much effort into their work as men in order to show their ability.

Women writers have recognized this inequality between the sexes. Writers like Zhang Jie, Zhang Xinxin, Zhang Kangkang, and Bai Fengxi are giving voice to the problem and expressing their discontent.

Deng Yaping, one of the top table tennis players in China.

Women in sports

Participating in sports for one's health is something that only began to develop in China in 1949. It had never been widespread among scholars, and very few girls played sports because of their bound feet. Effort has been put into developing sportsmen and women for competitive sports. Nevertheless, for every 3 million people there is only one sports stadium, and for every 5 million people only one gymnasium. Those who engage in sports in China represent only 31.7% of the entire population; only 9% of all Chinese women play some sport.

Although the numbers may be small, Chinese sportswomen have become known internationally. In swimming, diving, ping-pong, badminton, and basketball, they have had some success.

On September 16, 1991, at the 15th Asian Cycling Race, 22-year-old Zhou Lingmei broke the world record previously held by Soviet cyclist E. Saloumiaee.

Aerobics is now fashionable in Beijing. The center for this is the Beijing Lisheng Health City, which provides amenities for people seeking more impressive muscular bodies. Participants dance and swing to rhythmic music to keep fit. They also learn how to use weights. More than half the participants are women.

In China women are not quite "half of heaven," as Mao proclaimed. However, the role they have played even as a minority in the work force has been more than significant for the development of China. Those who have had the chance and opportunity to develop their talents have excelled. With economic reforms, more and more women will no doubt achieve success.

Barcelona Olympics

At the Olympic Games in Barcelona in 1992, China sent a delegation of 251 athletes to compete in 20 events. China won 16 gold medals, 22 silver medals, and 16 bronze medals. A number of these were won by women.

The Chinese women's swimming team won four gold medals and five silver medals. In diving, Fu Mingxia, who is five feet tall and weighs a mere 92 pounds, became the youngest champion in Olympic history when she won the gold medal in platform diving. She was 14. (See above right: Mingxia executing a dive at the Olympics.) Mingxia entered diving school at the age of 10, and at 13, she won the women's platform event at the World Championships in Perth in 1991.

In women's gymnastics Lu Li, 16, won the gold medal for the uneven bars after obtaining the first-ever perfect score for this event. (See right: Lu Li on the balance beam. She won a bronze on this apparatus.)

Zhang Shan, a 24-year-old markswoman, scored 223 hits to beat a field of male opponents in the mixed skeet shooting event, equalling the men's world mark. She was the first and possibly the only woman winner of the event, as there will be no mixed skeet competition in future Olympiads.

In table tennis, women players Deng Yaping and Qian Hong won gold and silver medals.

chapter four

Being Woman

The past 100 years have brought great changes in the status and role of women in China; changes have accelerated over the last 40 years, with the other changes in Chinese society.

Women are no longer confined to the home. Nor do they behave as meekly as Chinese women once did. More than 80% of women of working age in the cities have jobs outside the home. That adds up to more than 51 million women. It is now considered "normal" for women to work outside the home and unusual to do otherwise.

Today Chinese women have their rights written into the constitution, which stipulates equality for men and women. Women have the right of inheritance and children can take their mother's family name.

Women may go to mediation committees or the courts to complain about mistreatment by their husbands. This is something no woman would have dreamed of doing in the old China. Women may apply for divorce—again something unheard of in earlier times—and many do. Moreover, in the cities, among younger, better educated people, there is no longer the terrible stigma against divorced or widowed women.

The changes are enormous. Women are more confident, they are better educated, and they have some economic independence as well as social status. But social changes as great as these come with a price for women.

Opposite and right:
Young women enjoying an outing, and praying at a temple. Change for Chinese women has been tremendous, particularly over the past 40 years. It has become the norm for women to work outside the home whereas only 50 years ago, most women stayed home to take care of the children and the elderly.

While Article 48 of the constitution states that "women in China enjoy equal rights with men in all spheres of life, political, economic, cultural, and social, including family life," the reality of Chinese society is a long way from this.

For example, the working woman is an equal partner with men at work, but returns to an unequal share of domestic chores at home. Some husbands help; the majority, however, do not. Social services for working women are few and far between.

For rural women the inequality is even greater. Education and job opportunities for them are far fewer than for their urban sisters.

How does one address a Chinese woman?

From 1949 to approximately 1985, the common appellation was "comrade." One talked about "women comrades." With the economic reforms this situation has changed. Today it is common to address young women as *xiaojie* ("shee-ow-jie") or "miss" and older women as *taitai* or "madam." For educated women, the form of address may be *laoshi* meaning "teacher," or *nushi* meaning "ms." Forms of address such as "miss" or "madam" were for a long time considered bourgeois. Those who do not like to use these forms of address use the terms *shifu* meaning "master worker" or *dajie,* which means "elder sister" and is both polite and friendly.

Equality of the sexes for a minority

In the large cities, among the well educated minority, the attitude toward women has changed considerably. In government ministries, in science and technology, in tertiary institutions, in art, publishing and theater, well educated, competent and able women have attained leading positions. As we have seen in the previous chapter, in industry and agriculture many capable women have become managers and they are able to hold their own. On the basis of their work they are treated equally and respected by their male colleagues.

However, an enormous effort is needed to attain such success. Women who get to the top in their profession have to perform better than their male counterparts. Often they are only promoted when they reach their mid-40s or 50s.

In China educated and proficient women are treated seriously and are able to work comfortably with men without being treated as sex objects.

Successful women are comparatively well paid and their success brings honor to the family. Studies show, however, that women achievers have either their parents, parents-in-law, or relatives to help them, or they can afford to hire domestic help; this relieves them of most heavy domestic chores. Very often they have a husband who is willing to support his wife's career and is not necessarily ambitious for himself. Some of these women remain single.

The working woman and her dual role

For the overwhelming majority of urban Chinese women, life is a matter of surviving at least 10 hard years in a dual role of worker and wife-and-mother. Since 1949 it has become the norm for an urban Chinese woman to work. This was regarded as socially necessary, for to work was to take part in the revolution of Chinese society. It was said that by taking part in the revolution, women would be liberated.

First step toward liberation

After women "joined the revolution" in the 1950s, the family relationship became one of greater equality, with women making decisions or taking part in family decision making. Even parents came to accept this. The important factor in this change was a woman's economic power. She was no longer economically dependent on her husband.

But the price paid by women for the right to work was high. With few modern conveniences, household chores took much time and effort, so that women were toiling from early morning until late at night. Shopping for food meant standing in long lines at state-run markets.

The result was that work was

perfunctory, household chores were carelessly done, and there was no time to be with one's children. Many women felt conscience-stricken, especially if the children did not perform well and the teacher gave them bad grades.

Road building. Women are expected to work like men at the workplace. And when they go home, they are expected to take on their traditional role of wife and mother, cooking, washing, cleaning, and mending.

> **"When a man and a woman start a home it is the beginning of human life and the source of all happiness. It begins with the husband and wife, followed by parents and children, then brothers and sisters. All the success and failure of the family come from the woman."**
> —*from* **I Ching**

Working in a silk factory. Many women prefer to work outside the home. With modernization, this is made easier for them, as household appliances lighten the housework. But there is still inadequate social support for working parents.

1990s: Woman, work and be liberated

Since the 1980s, with economic reforms and the open-door policy, China has become more prosperous. Today, in the 1990s, people do not talk about revolution, but the thinking is still that women can be liberated only through work.

This has brought with it some domestic modernization, particularly in urban areas. In the cities, 80% of households now have washing machines and the number that cook with gas has risen. People now use refrigerators and electric fans, and some even have air-conditioners, video recorders, and other appliances. Buying daily food is easier, now that there are free markets besides the state markets. The amount of time spent on domestic chores has decreased.

Life is now somewhat more relaxed and people's demands are different. People spend more time on leisure activities.

The parent gets little support The parenting role is frequently seen as subordinate and inferior to the work role. Managers praise the mother who "thinks only of the common good and puts aside private affairs." Caring for children must not interfere with work.

> **A survey of 1,400 working women found that 85% of them spent three to four hours per day on domestic chores, compared to one to two hours for their husbands. Fifteen percent of these women were solely responsible for all household chores. According to another survey, 55% of women think their burden is still heavy.**

The attitude of employers is this: if a woman works, she should work like a man, but if she considers looking after her family more important, she should leave work and go home. But the majority of women want to work.

Discrimination against women

While the Chinese male may respect a woman superior at work, his attitude toward ordinary working women or women in his own home is quite different. The male sense of superiority is quickly translated into discrimination in dealing with these women.

Employment In the past all factories and government agencies throughout China were highly overstaffed. This was seen as a way of employing the large population, although it was inefficient. Making a profit or breaking even was not considered essential as there were government subsidies to rely on. But as China is now trying to establish a market economy, this has to change. The emphasis is now on efficiency and profitability. Excess staff is being dismissed throughout the country.

Many working women recruited earlier were neither trained nor educated. As most were caught with the burden of two jobs (at home and at work), very often neither was properly done. Thus many directors of enterprises do their best to have these women dismissed. Some target pregnant women as the first to go.

Large numbers of women were among the first to be laid off in the three heavy industrial enterprises in Shenyang city. In one enterprise, 90% of those laid off were women. According to a study of 660 enterprises in 11 provinces, 62% of all laid-off workers were women.

Because of the double burden of family and work, there are those who advocate that women "return home." The majority of women are opposed to this. They do not wish to return home to social isolation and economic dependence. Yet for many women already out of work, finding another job is not easy.

Studies reveal that women who have been declared redundant have become less confident. They hesitate to make decisions and are reluctant to visit friends and relatives because of the loss of face at losing their jobs. They also find they are no longer consulted about family decisions and have lost some of their rights in the family economy. Some women said that after they left their jobs, the burden of housework was even heavier because their husbands no longer helped at all. Others said that after leaving work they had less to talk about with their husbands and tensions between them increased.

Why employers do not want women

One of the main reasons employers do not want to employ young women graduates is that women cost too much. They will marry, become pregnant and take maternity leave of 56 days on full pay. When their children are small they may take frequent leaves of absence because children often become ill. The work unit also has to pay a bonus to mothers with only one child (in support of the one-child family planning policy).

Some organizations have hired women graduates provided they agree not to get married or become pregnant in the first two years of their contract.

Another reason why employers do not want to hire women is that their working life is shorter. Women retire at age 55 rather than the 60 for men.

Even women managers are sometimes not too keen to hire women. One woman manager of the Keli High Technology Corporation said frankly that although she was a woman, she wanted fewer women in her corporation. She found women to be the most difficult to deal with: they complain and nag, and cause problems over trivial matters.

Government regulations stipulate that no work unit should refuse employment to a woman graduate. In a situation where a male candidate has the same qualifications as a woman, preference should be given to the woman. In reality this does not happen. One young woman found that the enterprise where she was seeking employment set the entrance examination score for men at 100 points and for women at 160.

Higher education It is a well-established fact that some universities and colleges deliberately enroll more men than women. All college candidates take an entrance examination, and some colleges lower the acceptance grade for male candidates. The result is that some women with high scores are kept out and men with lower scores get in. This is particularly so in engineering and other courses in which men have been predominant. Female candidates have to be at the top of the list in the entrance examination results before they are even considered.

The number of women college students remains low. In Beijing University (one of China's most prestigious for the humanities) women account for only 33% of undergraduates and 20% of graduate students. In Qinghua University (famous for science and engineering) women make up only 22% of all graduate students.

Employment for women graduates Today even young women graduates have difficulty in finding employment. Starting in 1949 all university and college graduates were assigned work under an overall plan issued by the State Planning Commission. Everybody got a job on graduation regardless of whether the graduate and the workplace were satisfied with each other. In 1985 changes to the recruitment system began, and since 1988 a prospective employee goes to the workplace to be interviewed. Thus the workplace has a wider range to select from, and as a result women university graduates find difficulty in obtaining employment. This is true despite the fact that they may have better results than their male counterparts.

Not all professions refuse women graduates. In medicine, teaching, and finance there are insufficient graduates to meet the demand. The industries in which women have difficulty obtaining work are the maritime, machinery, electronics, foundry, boilermaking, power generation, and other strongly male-dominated fields.

Every year, after the initial recruitment, around 80% of women graduates do not have jobs. Gradually they do find employment, sometimes in the joint ventures with foreign companies; sometimes they become self-employed. Generally it takes about a year before they find full-time employment.

Discrimination in politics When the 13th National Congress of the Chinese Communist Party was held in March 1987, not one woman was elected to the Political Bureau, the major decision-making body in China. Of the 288 elected members of the Central Committee of the Chinese Communist Party, only 22 were women.

In the 1987 election to governing bodies at the county and township

levels, the number of women representatives went down in 12 provinces and municipalities. Only 5% of the responsible positions in provincial and county governments are held by women. In some areas there is not a single woman in county and township governments.

On the whole, discrimination against women is very real in China. This is being recognized. However, because of the deeply ingrained sense of male superiority, it will be well into the next century before this problem will begin to be overcome.

Woman technician in a power plant. In this and other traditionally male-dominated industries, women face discrimination.

Woman farmer with her baby and her prized ox (*above*), a sidewalk market in a rural town (*opposite*). Rural people feel they are second-class citizens.

Women in rural areas: Very unequal opportunities

One of the greatest inequalities that exists in China today is in the enforced difference of residential status between town and country. There are two types of residential status: one is urban and the other rural. Almost 80% of the Chinese population have rural residential status. Not even marriage to a city dweller can alter that. The only way that a young person in the vast rural areas of China can change residential status is to pass the university entrance examinations. For the overwhelming majority, particularly for young women, this is almost impossible.

Differences between city and rural residential status

Politically, economically, and socially, the differences between the two types of residential status are great.

On the economic side, people with

urban residential status are given cooking oil and grain rations (in the past the rations also included cotton fabric, sugar, soap, fish, pork, eggs, and other items) which are sold to them at subsidized prices. Rural people do not receive this benefit. One must have city residential status to be formally employed by government agencies and industrial and commercial enterprises in the cities.

Children from rural areas cannot go to elementary or secondary schools in the cities or townships. Nor can rural people be housed or receive free medical treatment in cities or towns.

Workers with urban residential status have state-paid old age pensions of at least 70% of their wages. They have medical benefits and sometimes a rebate for family dependents. The rural aged have none of these.

In elections, the votes of five people in rural areas are equal to the vote of one person in urban areas. This is to guarantee the leading role of the urban "working class."

Second-class citizens The Chinese Communists claim economic reasons for this double residential status. They contend that China does not have sufficient wealth to give its enormous population equal benefits. Naturally, those in the rural districts who have a high school education are dissatisfied.

They feel they are treated like second-class citizens.

With the economic reforms, however, there have been some changes that allow men and women without urban residential status to enter the cities and become temporary or contract workers. In the past this was forbidden; one had to have permission from the local Communist authorities to do so. Young women have thus entered the cities to become domestic workers or to work in the service industries. They have no rights, no medical care, and have to buy commercially-priced grain. The majority of rural women, however, remain in the villages. It is against this background that we must see rural women.

Girls in the rural areas have little opportunity for education. Instead, from a young age, they have to work in the fields and help in the house.

Life of rural women Life is still very basic for the majority of rural women who live away from the rural townships. The majority of them work in the fields. They also have to help collect firewood or gather weeds to feed the pigs, chickens, and ducks.

From about the age of 14, a girl has to learn to weed the wheat field or the rice paddy. If she is strong, she sometimes has to pedal the irrigation pumps, as there is no electricity.

When harvest time comes, she will learn to cut either the wheat or rice with a sickle.

During the period of the communes (1958–79), the heavier work and work which required greater skill was given to men who received more work points and more money. The most a woman ever received was 80% of a man's wage, the majority receiving only around 70%. Today, where families work their own land, young women and girls have to be able to do all the tasks.

Life is very hard in the countryside. In many villages there is no electricity. Fresh drinking water has to be fetched from wells or the river and carried in two heavy wooden buckets balanced on the shoulders by a bamboo pole. Washing is done on the banks of the rivers or streams.

In many places cotton has to be spun into thread, dyed with vegetable dye, and woven into cloth to make clothes for family members. Girls also learn embroidery, particularly in the economically backward areas. All these skills are passed on from mothers to daughters.

Then there is the family vegetable plot where vegetables, tobacco, sometimes cotton, and other necessities are grown. This has to be weeded and watered regularly, tasks often done by the mother and her daughter. Pigs and chickens have to be fed and taken to the market to be sold. Eggs are also sold for money to buy kerosene, thread, needles, and other necessities.

The culture of needlework in China

As Lian Xiaochun, in her book *Feelings on Needlework Culture,* writes so expressively:
"For thousands of years, laboring women have done most of the embroidery. Their low social status deprived them of any right to express their feelings directly in society. They had to express their love and hate through their needlework. It was their only area of freedom. Their happiness, anger, love and hatred became vivid designs behind the flowers, insects, and fish that inhabited their fantasy world....

"Needlework also embodies the image of the Chinese woman. A woman's value lay more in the work she could do than in her possessions or beauty, and the quality of her needlework was a measure of her capability....

"There are three aspects to needlework culture. The first might be called reproduction. Women naturally take responsibility for reproduction and embroidery plays an important role in the reproductive functions in society—in the proposals of marriage, in the wedding ceremony and then in the birth and upbringing of the offspring. As girls grew up they embroidered silk balls, handkerchiefs, belts, and pouches in preparation for their future homes....

"After marriage, the new wives start to prepare for the birth of the children. In the countryside in south and north China you could hardly find a child who was not wearing a pair of tigerhead shoes or a red embroidered stomach cover made by his mother or grandmother....

"The second aspect of needlework culture might be called serving. A woman's status at home and in society was always low: she had no right to speak in public or even in the family. But she was responsible for maintaining the dignity of the family. The family, and the husband's reputation in part, depended on the cleverness a woman showed in her work. There was a saying: 'If you want to know the wife at home, just look at the clothes the husband wears.' This extended to the family at large.

"The third aspect might be considered education, in that embroidery taught and conveyed cultural values."

Women in rural industry Today with the economic reforms in agriculture and the growth of surplus labor, young country women are finding jobs in the new rural industries or the service industries that are springing up all over the country. So far there are 15 million rural and township enterprises throughout China, and they now employ 35 million women, which is 40% of the entire work force in rural and township enterprises. The number of women of working age (16–54) in rural China is 181 million, so those employed in rural industry are still in the minority.

In these industries, women are mainly employed in food processing, silk weaving, the production of knitwear, clothing and traditional arts and crafts, industrial processing, and so on. In some of these enterprises capable women have become factory managers and directors.

Women in rural China still wear trousers as these are the most practical garment for women who work in the fields. In the past many girls wore a plain, blue cotton, high-necked jacket. This has given way to the Western-style shirt, often made in bright floral or checked material, and a plain jacket made of cotton or some synthetic material that is easy to wash and dry. In more remote areas Hakka women still wear black cotton tops and trousers and wide-brimmed hats, while other ethnic minorities wear their traditional clothes.

Changes in lifestyle In the more prosperous regions of China such as the provinces of Fujian and Guangdong, taking part in production has increased rural women's desire to study. In Guangdong province some 6 million women are enrolled in night schools for general education and technical studies.

A job in the rural industries means wages and access to other amenities provided by industrialization. Young women watch television and this influences them in many ways, such as in style of dressing and in attitudes toward life and society. Some no longer wish to wear their hair in long braids, but prefer to cut it or have a permanent so they can look like city women.

Changes, however, are not just in outward appearances, but also in their attitudes toward society. Many young women wish above all to be free to marry whom they please. Generally the more educated a young woman is, the less traditional her outlook. In rural China there are still a great many places where marriages are arranged and this custom is still widely accepted.

Domestic workers An old custom that has been revived with new-found wealth, brought about by economic reforms, is the use of domestic help. In the past women from rural areas entered the city to become domestic workers in wealthy families. They generally did the shopping, cooking, and cleaning.

Today, with the majority of women working, the need for domestic help is great. Where families can afford it, a domestic helper is hired to care for a small child, or to do the housework and cooking. They rarely do both. Or they may be employed instead to look after an ailing parent. They also work for the elderly or retired who need help with daily chores.

It has been calculated that in Beijing there are over 40,000 domestic workers and another 40,000 are needed. Shanghai employs some 60,000.

But the domestic workers of the 1980s and 1990s are nothing like those of the past, who were illiterate peasant girls expecting nothing more than a place to live and at least one meal a day.

Today's domestic workers may still be country girls, but their demands and life expectations are quite different. Most are between 17 and 25 years old and many of them are junior or senior high school graduates. Many have come to the cities to earn money for their dowries. Some have come with their books in the hope of continuing to study, so they can leave the rural areas altogether.

Domestics expect to enter a household with a color television, a refrigerator, and even a telephone. They also expect presents on arrival, like a wristwatch, as well as one when they leave, perhaps a wristwatch for their fiance. Often they eat with the family.

Their monthly wage ranges from $10 to $16 and is worth about the same as their board. It costs at least $16 to feed a person for a month. In all, this comes to around $32, which is as much as a university graduate receives monthly in the first year of work.

The domestic helpers often come from the rural areas where there is a shortage of land and a surplus of labor. Many come from areas of great poverty, where the local government encourages the young girls to go to the cities to find employment. Within a few years these young women have sent millions of dollars back to their home villages.

Today domestic service companies have been set up to arrange employment. In 1985 Shanghai opened a School for Domestic Workers.

Women carvers. Economic reforms mean that life for the rural girl need not be confined to farm work. She can work in the rural industries, for instance, making handicrafts, or she can go to work in the city in a textile factory or get a job as a domestic worker.

Female infanticide

The traditional Chinese concept that the "family line" can only be continued by a male heir is deeply rooted. The birth of a son was considered a great event, while the lack of one was considered a great misfortune. Over the centuries, female infanticide has been a common practice.

With the introduction of the one-child family planning policy in the 1980s, female infanticide has recurred. This reflects two problems, one of which is the Chinese attitude toward marriage. Marriage primarily serves to continue the family line, which is seen as a wife's role.

A Chinese father considers his family his property. Only he has the right to deal with the family as he sees fit. After some proven cases of female infanticide, the government had to explain to people why this is a criminal act. Under the law, an offender may be sentenced to three to 10 years' imprisonment.

However, there are still some cases of husbands abusing their wives, persecuting them, and even forcing them into a divorce so they can find another wife who will give them a son. There are some in-laws who will also molest and mistreat their son's wife because she has not produced a son. Such cases are found not only in outlying villages in the remote hinterland but also in the cities. Workers, peasants, Communist Party members, government officials—even fairly high-ranking ones—behave in this way.

Alternatively, parents use another tactic to get around the one-child policy. The 1990 national census shows that the number of female children over the age of five is higher than the number of registered female births five or six years earlier. Why is there a discrepancy? There is only one answer: baby girls have been hidden by their families. This allows families to try to have a son. In 1990 alone it has been estimated that there were approximately 600,000 girls who were unregistered. So far parents are not prosecuted when they have been found with more than one child. Government measures like stopping of work bonuses and higher school fees for the extra child are not working because of the economic reforms and the ensuing prosperity.

While female infanticide may have ceased, not registering baby girls in itself defeats the purpose of the family planning policy.

Age-old prejudices in rural areas China is an enormous country with 22% of the world's population. Some 220 million people live in cities and 800 million in the countryside.

While great advances have been made in the cities and in the countryside near the large cities, the majority of rural Chinese still live traditional lifestyles. Perhaps a highway, a dam, or a bridge may be built near them that will cause some changes, but on the whole changes are slow to occur.

Idea of male superiority The concept of male superiority remains strong in all rural areas. Women may no longer have bound feet but feudal ideas of chastity still remain—there are still those who insist that girls be examined before

> "Once, as I was weeding in the vegetable garden, two young girls from the village came to visit me....I gave them some surplus seedlings and they in turn helped me with my weeding. They referred to their menfolk as 'the big men.' Their marriages were arranged by their parents; girls as young as 12 or 13 had been promised in marriage. One girl pointed a finger at the other saying, 'She has been engaged and is expecting to be married soon.' Embarrassed, the latter retaliated and said, 'She has been promised in marriage to a family too.' Both were illiterate."
>
> —*Yang Jiang,* Six Chapters of Life in a Cadre School

marriage to show proof they are virgins. There is ignorance of the facts of life, including the fact that the male is the determinant of gender.

As can be seen, traditional ideas have not changed much.

Women are still subject to much abuse in that they are expected to submit to an arranged marriage.

Arranged marriages Today marriage for the rural woman is still an arrangement made between her parents and the family of the chosen husband-to-be.

In many areas marriage between relatives is still common. This is out of economic consideration, because families that know each other and that are related will not expect expensive betrothal presents and dowries, which can land a family in great debt. However, marriage between relatives is not a healthy practice, socially or genetically. Again ignorance and poverty remain the reasons for such practices.

For families in dire poverty, a daughter may be sold. Only 60 miles north of Guangzhou, in some poor villages, girls are engaged at an early age. For some 10 years the families of their future husbands send rice and sweet potatoes to the girl's family until the price is right, and then she is married off. Such parents refuse to send their daughters to school in case they learn about the outside world and may run away one day, leaving the family with a debt that they can never hope to repay.

In the countryside, traditional customs are still practiced, and marriages are arranged. Sometimes girls are engaged at a young age.

Some brides are bought

In many places there is a shortage of young women. Men make up 51.45% of the population. Also many young women with a high school education do not want to remain in the village and marry the average rural male. This has resulted in abuses such as the sale of brides.

In 1989 the average price for a bride in Hebei province, brought in from outside the local area, was $531.40. The highest price was $800 and lowest $10 for an eight-month-old baby.

In a survey of 178 girls sold in Hebei, it was found that 63% were illiterate.

The problem does not lie so much in the buying and selling of girls as brides. Worse, there are big rackets run by criminal gangs that kidnap and sell young girls. Some are even kidnapped and sold to brothels in Taiwan. From November 1989 to the end of October 1990, police rescued 10,000 kidnapped girls throughout the country.

Hopes of young women Today many young women who have managed to graduate from junior or senior high school want to leave the villages for the towns not only to work but also to be free. Some want to study more, and most hope to find a husband who will not chain them to ignorance and poverty. This is causing much friction and difficulty between the young women and their families, although some families are understanding of the problem.

The problem is made worse because when young women go to the cities having only rural residential status, they are vulnerable and may not necessarily find long-term employment.

Women of ethnic minority

There are 56 ethnic minority groups in China which according to the 1990 national census make up 8.9% of the population in China. Han Chinese, who are the dominant ethnic group, have long had a policy of assimilation of the ethnic minorities. For centuries the Chinese have regarded themselves as superior people and the bearers of higher civilization to primitive peoples. For that reason, there has been little respect for the customs and religions of minorities in China.

Under the present regime the authorities have aided the advancement of the minorities by providing them with schools, hospitals, and factories. They have allowed some of their cultural heritages to be retained, including ethnic costumes and traditional housing. Chinese laws are binding on all minorities, including the Marriage Law, which bans polygamy and polyandry.

Ethnic minority women have been trained in Chinese colleges and universities to encourage economic and social

Dai women of southwestern China. There are 56 ethnic minority groups in China. Most of the minority peoples live in poverty in rural areas.

changes among their own people. Some have become nurses, Red Cross workers, accountants, teachers, and government workers. Such workers have become sinicized, that is, Chinese in their outlook, language, culture, and values.

Ethnic minorities live in a wide area, both in the hinterlands and the border regions. For the majority of women in rural areas, changes have come slowly.

Mongolian women

Mongolians live in Inner Mongolia and are scattered through other parts of northern China. They remain a nomadic people and in China the majority receive very little education. There are only 2 million Mongolians in Inner Mongolia. Eighteen million Han Chinese now live in Inner Mongolia and continue to expand and encroach farther and farther onto the grasslands. The policies of the Han Chinese threaten and are destroying the traditional livelihood and culture of the Mongolians. Moreover, the Mongolians are bound by Chinese law to practice family planning and birth control, and limit themselves to only one child per family. The Mongolians practice Tibetan Buddhism.

A Mongolian woman lives in a yurt, a circular tent made of skins or felt, stretched over a framework, with her family, which usually includes her husband, her children and her mother-in-law.

In the past, it was often the custom for a man and a woman to live together without marrying. The man would help the woman with work like setting up the yurts and slaughtering animals for winter food. He would perhaps leave her after a period of time. If a child was born, it took the mother's surname.

Mongolian women lead a hard life.

water, and makes tea with mare's milk. Breakfast consists of a big bowl of tea and the meat left over from the previous night's meal. Then the sheep and horses are taken to graze. While watching over them, the woman makes rope from wool or horse hair or sew clothes from skins. Her children may be with her, in which case the schoolteacher will come by on horseback and tutor the children then ride off to another family. At dusk the woman brings the sheep home and lights the fire to prepare the evening meal that is generally boiled lamb or beef.

When autumn comes, enough sheep and an ox must be killed to provide winter food for the family. After the animals are slaughtered, the woman and her mother-in-law have to skin, cut, then store the meat in the skin of the cleaned-out stomach of the ox. This parcel is then left outside to freeze. On the grasslands in winter the temperature goes down to $-22°F$.

In the old days, women had to give birth outside the yurt in the sheep pen, because having babies was thought to be an unclean act. In the extreme sub-zero temperatures, many babies died. Today women are able to have children in hospitals.

Women work hard and are respected, particularly as they grow older, but male dominance and female inferiority remain unchanged for the majority of Mongolian women on the grasslands. Changes are slow in coming.

The custom today, however, is for husbands and wives to live together. A family generally has two or more yurts, 50 head of cattle and 700 sheep. They are constantly on the move, living where there is water and grass. To stay in a place any longer than 10 days is considered a long time. Instead, they move to places where the grass is fresh, which means taking down the yurts. Every beam of wood has to be placed in order on a cart, and a family will have as many as 14 wooden carts on which everything is loaded. They will then make their way slowly across the grasslands to a new grazing place.

A day in the life of a woman on the grasslands is very hard. She is awake from dawn to dusk and even has to keep watch at night in case wolves attack the sheep.

Rising at dawn, she lights the stove using dried cow dung for fuel, boils the

Mongolian marriage

Mongolian marriages are generally arranged through the parents, although the young people have met before. This varies in different localities.

The marriage celebration is an important part of Mongolian culture. The people of the grasslands live a hard and lonely life and a marriage is a happy community celebration. On the day of the wedding, the bridegroom and a group of young men go to the bride's home. They are stopped at the door of the yurt; they cannot enter. The singer of the bride's family will ask: "Who are you? Why have you come?" and the groom's singer will reply. The questions and answers go on until they have all been satisfactorily answered.

Finally the groom and his entourage are allowed to enter the yurt. They are feted, sometimes for two or three days, sometimes for half a day. When it is time to take the bride, she sits in the midst of her sisters and friends who sing that they want to keep her a little longer. As she leaves, her mother sings a song called *Mother Instructs Her Daughter*, in which she exhorts her daughter to respect her parents-in-law and cooperate with her husband.

The daughter replies with a song that says it is the destiny of a girl to be married.

Before she leaves, young men who have been attracted to the girl and would have liked to marry her sing of their love. Sometimes this is very sad.

Then the bride and groom mount their horses and ride back across the grasslands to the bridegroom's home. They are accompanied by their relatives, so there are many, many people riding across the prairie.

At the groom's home, a huge banquet is held, where singers from the two families improvise songs with questions and responses. Many of the songs ask questions about history, geography, and legend, all of which have to be answered.

The bride has to stand by herself for the entire wedding feast. She stands in her wedding dress with a magnificent headdress. The wealthier the bridegroom's family, the richer the headdress. The bridegroom helps look after the guests. The merrymaking goes on for as long as three days, with the bride standing the entire time.

Over the past 30 years the Communists had forbidden these customs, which meant the near destruction of an integral part of the culture of the Mongolian people. Today, however, these customs are being revived. (The picture above shows two women preparing the wedding clothes of their brother-in-law.)

Uygur woman reading a newspaper in the Uygur language (*above*) and a Kirghiz woman (*opposite*). The people of Xinjiang are mainly herders living a nomadic life. But the government has set up herder settlements so that families can lead a more settled life. Women appreciate the advantages of these settlements.

People of Xinjiang

There are over 6 million people of Uygur (wee-goor) nationality who live around the Tianshan Mountains and the Tarim Basin in China's far northwest. This is known as the Xinjiang Uygur Autonomous Region.

The language of the Uygurs is close to Turkish and their religion is Sunni Islam. The area they live in is very dry, but there are many oases that enable the people to live as farmers. The Uygurs grow cotton, wheat, corn, and rice. They are also famous for the cultivation of white seedless grapes.

There are many other ethnic minorities who live in Xinjiang together with the Uygurs. These are the Hui (Moslem) Mongolians, Kazakhs, Kirghiz, Uzbeks, Salars, and Tajiks, to name a few. Many are herders, living a nomadic life much like the Mongolians.

Livestock is the main source of rural household income. Women play a major role in livestock management, including sheep, dairy cattle, pigs, poultry, and rabbits.

The Xinjiang Women's Federation, a branch of the All-China Women's Federation, has been an important force in bringing changes to the life of women in Xinjiang.

Its policies promote the right of women to work outside the home. The federation also offers a number of production-oriented training classes for herders and other people. In some counties, these classes include training women in livestock and pasture management, cotton-growing, corn production, rice production, pig and chicken raising, dress-making, and handicrafts.

In the Tianchi area, a famous scenic spot, the local women's federation hopes

Herder settlement

The Chinese have established large farm settlements so that herding families can become settled. Fukang county, north of Urumqi (capital of Xinjiang), is the foremost county for settlement, with over 200 households.

Most women herders who have settled on farms feel the biggest benefit has been their children's better access to schooling. In Fukang county, school enrollment exceeds 98%. Before settlement, some mothers had arranged for their children to live with other people nearer the school. But now they live with their children and are happier because they are all together.

For women the other advantages of settlement include the ability to cultivate pasture, to give their children access to off-farm employment, to be closer to hospital facilities, and to have access to television. Also, life in a fixed dwelling is less tiring than constantly moving a yurt. The house is warmer, fuel can be delivered and stored, and access to water is easier.

Doctors have found that after living in permanent housing, herders are less likely to suffer from influenza and rheumatism and their diet improves as they eat more vegetables and fruit, rather than just meat.

Women now enjoy more frequently social gatherings. Social visits between households are more easily arranged.

All these social changes in the long run affect the traditional lifestyles of these ethnic peoples, particularly with regard to young women. Many of them, having access to education, will go to universities, colleges, and technical training institutes and will demand a complete break with the tradition of being married off at their parents' discretion. They will also demand employment and freedom of choice in marriage.

to improve the economic situation of Kazakh herdswomen by developing tourism and tourist-oriented handicrafts.

Women officials often travel by horse, bicycle, or sometimes by farm vehicle, to visit women in scattered herding sites in the mountains.

They deliver birth control pills and sometimes hold seven- to 10-day training classes in the mountains. These are usually about caring for livestock, children's education, and family planning.

Women's country

The Mosuo people are another of China's minorities. They live in southwestern China by Lake Lugu in Sichuan province. This area is known as "women's country." Their family structure is that of a large matriarchal family with lineage passed down via the mother.

Here, men and women are not married in a formal ceremony. As long as a man and a woman from different families feel affection for each other, they can have an *axia* ("ah-sia") relationship that can last for as little as a few months or as long as several years, or even a lifetime. *Axia* means "lover" or "sweetheart."

In the evening, an adult woman admits her *axia* into her bedroom, and in the morning the man returns to his own house. This is called "walking marriage" because the man has to walk to his *axia*'s home to meet her. A man and a woman can be united freely, and they can separate freely as well. If the woman refuses to admit the man into her bedroom in the evening, or the man does not go to the woman's house for a period of time, the relationship is considered over. Any children come under the mother's care; the father has no obligation to raise or support the children.

Yi women

There are over 6 million Yi people who live mainly in western Sichuan on the Liangshan Mountains. Some also live in Yunnan province, in the far southwest of China. They used to live in the fertile valleys, but over the centuries, as the Chinese population grew, it drove the minorities from their ancient lands up into the mountains. The Yi people live on the lower slopes and breed sheep. They are very poor. Prior to 1958 the Yi nationality practiced slavery, but this has since been abolished.

The story of Ya Ya Some of the marriage customs of the Yi people were harsh and unfair to women. Marriages were arranged, and when a man died, his brother or his father, if there were no brothers, could marry his widow. Yi people betrothed their daughters at an early age, very often to relatives.

The story of Ya Ya, which took place in the 1980s, tells vividly of the enormous difficulties young women have to overcome to choose their own marriage partners.

As a child Ya Ya was engaged to her cousin Mo Ya. She went to school when she was 11, but Mo Ya, who was five years older, stayed in the village to work the land because his father had died.

When Ya Ya finished primary school her parents wanted her to marry. But she wanted very much to study accounting, so her parents and her aunt, Mo Ya's mother, agreed to postpone the marriage. When she graduated at 20, Ya Ya was again pressured to marry. She had no affection for Mo Ya, but she agreed to the wedding ceremony, provided she did not live with Mo Ya for a time.

After she began working, Ya Ya learned about the disadvantages of marriage between close relatives. She also felt acutely the differences between herself and Mo Ya, who was semi-literate. When her aunt continued to press that she live with Mo Ya, she decided to break the marriage contract. The opposition she encountered from both families and the villagers was strong. How could she, a young woman, go against tradition in such a way?

Once a drunk Mo Ya broke into Ya Ya's room, threatening to explode a bomb and kill them both if she continued to live apart from him. Then one day, while in another township, Mo Ya got drunk again and was killed at a railway crossing.

Her aunt now demanded that Ya Ya marry Mo Ya's brother. Ya Ya refused, and finally the aunt agreed to nullify the contract if Ya Ya paid her $600 as compensation. Ya Ya wanted to take her to court, but was stopped by her father. In the end she gave her aunt $220.

Then her father told her he would no longer interfere in any plans she might have for marriage, but she must pay him $420 for raising her.

In 1984, Ya Ya was introduced to Mu Nai, a doctor, who had renounced his engagement to his cousin. Ya Ya and Mu Nai fell in love with each other and married.

There are many stories like Ya Ya's, not all with such a happy ending. Many young women commit suicide and even more young women enter unhappily into an arranged marriage. In the vast areas of rural China there is still a long way to go to implement the Marriage Law. The obstacles lie in the centuries-old customs, habits, and traditions which are deeply ingrained in both men and women. It is only when women themselves become educated and are able to discern these problems and demand that the law protect them that there will be a change to such customs.

Yi women like other minority women are bound by old customs that can be harsh and unfair to women.

Education for daughters of ethnic minorities

The education of ethnic minority girls is no easy task. Besides poverty and the remoteness of their homes, centuries-old prejudices against girls studying remain strong. The work done here by teachers is a tribute to their devotion to their profession and their high sense of duty.

In Gansu province, in northwestern China, lying between the Loess and Qinghai plateaus, is the Linxia Hui Autonomous Prefecture. There are a number of nationalities here—the Hui, Dongxiang, Sala, Tu, Tibetans, Uygur, and Han Chinese. The place is very poor and backward. Thirty-six percent of the people do not have enough to eat or wear; 50% between the ages of 12 and 40 are illiterate; only 76.1% of the children are enrolled in schools, compared with the national average of 97.2%. Eighty-three percent of the children not enrolled in school are the daughters of ethnic minority families. In some towns only three out of every 10 girls go to school.

One of the difficulties that has to be overcome in sending these girls to school is the custom that a girl of 13 must stay with her mother and should not mix with boys outside the home. This is particularly so for Moslem girls. In one township it was decided to go with tradition and run an all-girls class. The only female teacher, Ma Yuping, of the Hui nationality (Chinese Moslem), was put in charge of this experimental class. When news spread that a 40-year-old Hui woman would be responsible for the class, 70 girls between the ages of 5 and 11 were enrolled.

For three years Ma Yuping taught this all-girls class. Later three newly-graduated female teachers were added. Discipline was no problem, but the girls had grown up in an illiterate environment and found learning extremely difficult. By the time the girls had reached the second grade, 30 of them had left school for various reasons.

However, by 1987, the prefecture had established 36 all-girls classes with a total enrollment of 1,122.

To improve education for girls, the prefecture has taken a series of measures that include collecting educational funds in the prefecture, punishing parents who refuse to send their daughters to school

> It is a common thing for teachers to describe their class as: "Full in spring, halved by summer, down to several in fall and none in winter."
> This is because in spring there is enough to eat and the weather is warm. In summer, some of the children leave because of the shortage of food. In autumn most have to help their families as much work has to be done in the fields. In winter, they stay at home because they have too few clothes to protect them from the severe winter cold.

with much heavier fines than those who refuse to send boys, and setting up boarding facilities for schoolgirls in the third grade and above.

Conditions are hard in this part of China, but there are those who have the foresight and determination to see to the education of a whole new generation. To them this is the only way the deep-rooted ancient prejudices of race and sex can be eliminated.

How liberated are Chinese women?

How liberated, how equal are Chinese women with men? The constitution and other laws guarantee the equality of the sexes. The law stipulates equal pay for equal work and that women have equal working rights.

In 1990, more than 51 million women worked in urban areas, making up 38% of the total urban work force. They total 40% of the work force in rural industries (35 million). But does the widespread employment of women guarantee equality of the sexes? The official line is that if women work, then they are equal to men. But women still do the household chores at home, thus shouldering a double burden.

The emphasis on equality of the sexes has been solely in the workplace. No one has addressed the problem of how the traditional work of women is to be done equally in the home.

The constitution clearly stipulates

that men and women should enjoy equal rights in education. In fact these rights are far from equal. Women account for over 70% of China's illiterates. In 1991, of the 3 million school-age children unable to go to school, 83% were girls.

So where is the equality? It has failed to materialize in greater opportunities for women in the work force, for women in politics, or for women in education. It has failed to materialize in the form of more day care centers and nurseries, after-school care, and other social support for working women. The reality is women are far from equal.

Learning the Koran. Minority girls face great obstacles in receiving an education. Besides the remoteness of their homes, there is strong prejudice against girls studying.

chapter five

Profiles of Women

T here have been many outstanding women throughout the ages in China, despite the continual repression they have suffered. It is only in the 20th century that more women have had the opportunity to develop their talents, especially since 1949 when more women began to have the chance to be educated and to build a career. In this chapter we look at some women who have made their mark on Chinese society.

Song Qingling

Just before her death in 1981, Song Qingling ("sohng ching-ling") was given the title honorary president of the People's Republic of China. From 1949 until she died, she was vice-president. Song Qingling's story depicts the life of a woman dedicated to China.

Qingling is one of the three Song sisters who are known even in the West for the parts they played in China's history. The eldest sister, Song Ailing, married a banker, a descendant of the family of Confucius. Qingling, the second sister, married the founder of the Republic of China—Sun Yat-sen. The youngest sister, Meiling, married the man who led the Nationalists against the Communists—Chiang Kaishek.

Ailing is said to have drained the country of its wealth and Meiling is said to have wooed the United States to obtain aid for expensive Nationalist campaigns against the Communists. In China it was said that Ailing loved money, Meiling loved power, but Qingling loved China.

Members of the Young Pioneers (*opposite*) and a performer at a parade (*right*). Young girls who aspire to accomplish things in life are not short of role models.

Schoolgirl years Song Qingling was born in 1893 in Shanghai into an atypical Chinese family. Her father Charlie Song was educated in North Carolina where he was baptized a Methodist. He returned to Shanghai in 1886, where he became a very successful businessman. Qingling's mother was also an educated Christian. Qingling and her sisters received a Western education.

In 1908 at the age of 15, Qingling went to Wesleyan College in Macon, Georgia. Qingling and her sisters were the first Chinese girls to go to America to study. They did not have their feet bound, they did not have their marriages arranged, and they all spoke and wrote excellent English. This emancipation from the narrow rigidity of Chinese society enabled Qingling to have a broader vision of China's place in the world.

In America Qingling majored in philosophy and was for a time literary editor of the school magazine. At the age of 18 she wrote an article for the college magazine, the *Wesleyan*, in which she expressed her deep desire to reform China. In this essay she also attacked the system of arranged marriage, believing that its abolition would further liberate both men and women. The ideal of a new and better China remained always in her heart, inspiring her for the next 70 years.

Life with Sun Yat-sen Qingling's father worked closely with Sun Yat-sen, the first President of the Republic of China and founder of the Nationalist Party. Thus, Qingling got to meet Sun.

On October 25, 1915, Song Qingling married Sun Yat-sen, after running away from home to join him in Japan. He was 49, she was 22.

Sun had abdicated the presidency in favor of Yuan Shihkai in 1912. A year after the death of Yuan in 1916 Sun went to Canton (Guangzhou) in southern China, where he was elected head of a new republican military government. In the north the warlords were in control, so there was no national government then. A group of militarists in Canton rebelled against Sun, and he and Qingling were forced to flee to Shanghai. It was at this time she had a miscarriage.

In November 1924, the Suns were invited to Beijing by the new regime. They traveled by boat via Japan. In

> **It was hero-worship from afar. It was a romantic girl's idea when I ran away to work for him—but a good one. I wanted to help save China and Dr. Sun was the one man who could do it. So I wanted to help him.**
> —*Song Qingling on her romance with Sun Yat-sen*

Nagasaki Qingling gave one of her major addresses on the emancipation of women.

Sun arrived in Beijing a very sick man in January 1925, and died on March 12.

His last words were: "Peace, struggle, save China…"

Song Qingling remained faithful to his words for the rest of her life.

Years of struggle What followed were many years of hardship. She was forced into exile in Russia from 1925 to 1931, during which her own health suffered.

From 1931 to 1937 she lived in Shanghai, where she continued to devote herself to questions of national importance. The Nationalist regime was repressive and intolerant of dissent. Qingling was constantly under surveillance. In 1932, with a group of eminent cultural figures, she set up an organization called the China League for Civil Rights. One of the women members was abducted and the Secretary of the League was murdered. The League then collapsed. Nevertheless, Qingling used her position to try to get information out of China to the outside world and arouse solidarity abroad.

Qingling was elected vice-president of the World Committee Against Fascism that was founded in Paris in 1933. Very daringly, she convened a clandestine conference in Shanghai in September 1933—the Far East

Qingling and Sun Yat-sen. Qingling believed Sun was the man who could save China, and she wanted to help him.

Conference of the World Committee Against Imperialist War.

By 1931 the Japanese had invaded northeastern China. In 1937 Qingling made a strong appeal to the Nationalist Central Executive Committee for a united front with the Communists. In July 1937, the Japanese launched an all-out attack on central and southern China. The Nationalists had to reach an agreement with the Communists. A united front was formed.

After the surrender of Japan in 1945, Qingling appealed for a coalition government between the Nationalists and the Communists, to no avail.

Happier times. Qingling with Lei Jieqiong, president of the Society for Research and Marriage and the Family. During the Cultural Revolution, Qingling, like other Chinese, suffered at the hands of the Red Guards. Only her international fame protected her from greater harm.

Vice-president of China The civil war in China, which lasted from 1947 to 1949, resulted in Communist victory and the establishment of the People's Republic of China. Qingling was given many posts, the most important of which was as one of the vice-presidents of the Republic. Her role was honorary and symbolic.

Qingling was active in the official women's movement. She was honorary president of the All-China Women's Federation from the time of its founding. She spent most of her time in welfare work. She organized the China Welfare Institute, focusing on the welfare of children. This organization published an English-language periodical, *China Reconstructs*, which she founded in 1952.

More difficult years After 1957 there was a long period of repression aimed mainly at intellectuals. The Cultural Revolution began in 1966, and Red Guards desecrated the Song family grave in Shanghai. They pasted slogans and posters on the walls of Qingling's residence in Beijing, condemning her and the Song family. She and her staff reacted by putting up, in enormous characters that covered a whole wall, the slogan "Long Live the Great Leader Chairman Mao." The Red Guards did not dare destroy this, and there were no more posters.

As any attack on Song Qingling could have serious international repercussions, the then Premier Zhou Enlai had the Song family grave restored and gave Qingling protection. However, some of the staff sent by the government to care for her treated her with cold disdain. She suffered other tragedies, such as the suicide of her cousin.

Relief from fear The Cultural Revolution ended in 1976 and Song Qingling, like millions of other Chinese, experienced relief from fear for the first time in many years. Suffering from illness, Qingling made her last public appearance in early May 1981, when she received an honorary doctorate of law from Victoria University in Canada. Four days later she wrote her last words—an inscription for a book containing the manuscripts of Chinese patriot Chou Tao-jen. She died on May 29, 1981, at the age of 88. Her remains were placed, as she had instructed, in the family tomb in Shanghai, next to her parents and a lifelong servant.

Qingling was a beautiful woman, both dignified and serene, who dressed very plainly and lived simply. She did not seek power or fame, and lived her life devoted to the ideal of a better China; a China where she hoped there would be less suffering for the people. She remained a widow, devoted to the ideals of her husband, Sun Yat-sen. A warm person with great compassion for humanity, she is remembered as one of modern China's best daughters.

> There is one duty which men alone owe to themselves and the womenfolk. The law of equality can be written into historical documents for all to read. The fact of its existence can be widely publicized. There can even be some advancement on the part of women towards this equalization. But all of this will be voided unless the doctrine of equality is thoroughly thought out by the men and held in their firm grip. We women have evidence of many men who are progressive in other matters, even to the extent of risking their lives for the people's cause, but who persist in clutching to their antiquated ideas regarding women. This has an unwholesome and repressive effect and must be completely exposed.
> —*Song Qingling, December 11, 1949, in a speech at the Asian Women's Conference*

Jiang Qing

Jiang Qing was born Li Shuming in Shantung province in 1914. She came from a very humble background. When she was a child she knew Kang Sheng, who was later to become the head of the Communist secret service.

As a girl she was rebellious. As a young woman, she was highly ambitious. Through Kang Sheng, she met a young Communist militant by the name of Yu Qiwei and lived with him for a short time. He introduced her to Marxist theories and politics in art. In 1933 she joined the Chinese Communist Party. Not long after, Yu Qiwei was arrested by the Nationalists.

Left alone and having a passion for acting, she went to Shanghai, where she changed her name to Lan Ping. She performed on stage and also taught at a workers' night school. She was arrested by the Nationalists, interrogated, and after signing a declaration denouncing Communism, was released. For the following two years she acted in some left-wing films and married an actor. However, she very soon left him, and in July 1937 made her way to Yanan, the central base of the Communists. There she met her former mentor, Kang Sheng, who was now very high up in the Communist hierarchy. He enrolled her in the party school.

Marriage to Mao At the lectures Mao Zedong gave, Lan Ping always came in late with books under her arm and her jacket thrown over her shoulders. Instead of sitting quietly at the back, she would go and sit in the front, attracting a lot of attention. When the lecture ended she would go up to Mao to ask questions.

This attracted the Chairman's attention. There were not many women in Yanan at the time, and although Mao knew most of them and would nod and say hello to each one he met during his evening stroll, or even dance with them at the weekend dance parties, no woman could approach him and chat with him as freely.

It was about this time that she changed her name to Jiang Qing. Mao Zedong appointed her secretary in the archives of the Military Commission. His office adjoined hers; not long after she became his mistress and was soon pregnant.

The other leaders of the time made inquiries into her background and discovered that she had been arrested and released by the Nationalists. It could only mean she had betrayed the Communists or that she was working for the Nationalists. However, Mao insisted on marrying Jiang Qing. The leaders decided to accept the marriage on the condition that Jiang Qing take no part in politics. Mao divorced his third wife to marry Jiang Qing.

Persecuting enemies In 1949, when the People's Republic was established, most Chinese had not heard of Jiang Qing. It was only with the outbreak of the Cultural Revolution that she became prominent.

The Cultural Revolution was launched by Mao to wrest power from other leaders who were overriding him. The struggle was bitter.

Jiang Qing used the Revolution to purge anyone who knew of her past. "Dig deeply into the black line of the '30s!" she instructed the Red Guards. Defenseless people who knew of her former relationships with other men and of her earlier marriage were relentlessly persecuted. These included the elderly maid who had served her and her first husband.

Those who knew of her betrayal to the Nationalists were imprisoned in solitary confinement, some for as long as eight years. Under labels such as "bourgeois," "capitalist roader," and "traitor," she got rid of anyone who displeased her. These people had to go to the countryside to work in the fields. In the name of the Revolution, people could be arrested and homes could be searched at any time, day or night.

The terror spread throughout the entire nation. There was no law, no government body to protect the people. Gradually, from believing she was bringing revolutionary thoughts and ideas to the masses, people throughout

Red Guards at a political rally. Jiang Qing made use of the Red Guards to persecute her enemies.

China began to hate Jiang Qing as they saw the results of her bitter campaigns.

If in the past Jiang Qing had been merely despised by some veterans of the Communist Party as a woman of loose virtue with a shady past, she had now made many enemies. In 1976 Beijing was full of talk about her lifestyle, her lovers past and present, and above all, her abuse of power.

Hunger for power As Chairman Mao grew older and weaker, Jiang Qing made plans to usurp the chairmanship of the Communist Party. After Mao's death on September 9, 1976, just before National Day on October 1, a large photograph appeared in the *People's Daily* of Jiang Qing standing in the center of the Chinese leadership. Everyone knew what she was planning. Fortunately, however, she and her cronies were arrested, and thus a 10-year reign of terror ended.

Jiang Qing wanted power. She was no feminist working to alleviate the hard lives of Chinese women. Her way of reforming the arts and literature was to cut out everything she did not approve of, with the result that the Chinese cultural scene became a veritable desert. For almost 10 years there was nothing to listen to other than the "eight model operas" she allowed. Books could not be published without her approval. At one stage, women were even expected to wear the dress she designed.

In education she abolished the classroom. Young people had to go to the countryside or factories to work with peasants and workers. This was called going to the classroom of society. As a result, an entire generation lost the opportunity to attend school.

The final years When Jiang Qing was arrested, the attendants who had served her spat on her. She was notorious for being temperamental, paranoid, and difficult. She even had a nurse locked up for a year because she had let the temperature in her room fall too low.

In a sense, Jiang Qing was a scapegoat for the atrocities of the Cultural Revolution. Nevertheless, she earned the enmity of the people through her own actions.

Jiang Qing remained in Beijing Qin-cheng prison until the mid-1980s. After that she was kept under house arrest until she committed suicide in 1991.

There have been great distortions, lies, and slander about me. What kind of Chinese Communist Party member would I be if the enemy did not attack me? To cite one example, during the battles in northern Shaanxi I was continuously doing political work in the army. Yet some have said that I was making shoes. Some others have said that as soon as I saw my first three lice in Yanan, I ran away. Actually, they don't know that I had lice again when I marched with the troops. In those days having lice was revolutionary!

—*Jiang Qing*

Zhang Zhixin

Zhang Zhixin ("jhang jhih-shin") is known throughout China as a heroine.

Zhang Zhixin was a Communist, an ordinary party official who worked in the cultural section of the Propaganda Department of the Liaoning Provincial Committee of the Chinese Communist Party in northeastern China.

She had been educated at the Chinese People's University in Beijing. She was married and had a daughter.

During the terror of the Cultural Revolution she dared to voice her doubts about what was happening throughout the country, and openly questioned the policies which were coming from Beijing, from Jiang Qing and Lin Biao (then minister of defense). For this she was executed.

Speaking her mind As the Cultural Revolution deepened, Zhang Zhixin saw many of the older Communists who had fought for a new China against the Japanese invasion and in the civil war, and who had worked tirelessly to rebuild the country, being paraded in the streets with dunce caps, publicly beaten, humiliated, and abused. She was troubled by this and questioned such actions.

Society was in chaos. At the time there was no law and the Red Guards did whatever they liked, which included the destruction of buildings and equipment, all in the name of revolution.

Zhang Zhixin was executed for questioning the policies of the Cultural Revolution.

Opposite: Jiang Qing speaking in her own defense during her trial in December 1980.

This sickened her, as it did most Chinese.

Zhang Zhixin openly questioned whether these policies coming from Beijing were correct, and if people like Jiang Qing and Lin Biao were genuine. She was extremely brave in doing so. Most people dared not even tell their husbands or wives for fear of exposure, so terrifying was the situation.

At a May Seventh Cadre School Zhang Zhixin was sent to work in the countryside under guard, at a May Seventh Cadre School. These were special "schools" in the countryside where government employees and intellectuals were sent to work with and learn from peasants.

Zhang Zhixin was subjected to struggle meetings, which were sessions in which the accused was questioned and criticized in front of all the people in their workplace.

A struggle meeting during which an accused is made to wear a placard which denounces him as a political enemy of Mao. His hair is being cut to denote that he is in the same category as a criminal. Zhang Zhixin was subjected to similar humiliation and criticism.

Zhang Zhixin stood her ground. She spoke openly against the chaos in China and the factional fighting, some of which involved the use of firearms.

This was in August 1969. She was ordered to admit that she was wrong and to confess that she was against the Communist Party. She was placed under guard and forced to write her confession. Instead of doing so, she wrote out her own viewpoint and insisted she was right.

For this she was taken to prison, where she was allowed access to books. She read, made notes, and even wrote poetry. Because she refused to confess, she was brutally tortured. Later, she was taken back to the May Seventh Cadre School and made to stand for hours in the freezing cold of –4°F.

Execution On August 24, 1974, Zhang Zhixin was sentenced to life imprisonment for "counter-revolutionary crimes." In prison she continued to say what she thought and refused to admit her guilt. She was tortured even more brutally, and on April 3, 1975, she was sentenced to death. Her execution was carried out immediately. No appeal was permitted. She was 45 when she was executed. While in prison she wrote,

"Time and reality will pass just
   judgement,
Victory will greet the spring."

Rehabilitation In 1979, three years after the end of the Cultural Revolution, Zhang Zhixin's case was reviewed. Her story was published in the *People's Daily*.

The reaction throughout China was tremendous. Even the *People's Daily* did not dare publish in detail how brutally she was tortured. Her writings were heavily edited.

In a country with one-party rule, people are not encouraged to think clearly and speak their minds the way Zhang Zhixin did. She genuinely, almost naively, believed in her ideals, that "a Communist should always be upright, frank, outspoken." Her bravery is greatly admired, even if most people dare not emulate her.

Lin Qiaozhi

Lin Qiaozhi ("chi-ao-je") was born in Fujian province in 1901 and was brought up a Christian. When she was five, her mother died, and she lived with relatives in a big extended family. When she was a child, an elder aunt would braid her hair. "She always did it hurriedly," Lin Qiaozhi said, "because she had her own children to look after. She was good to me, but it's not the same as having one's own mama to braid one's hair, is it? From that time on, I felt I wanted to do something for mothers and not let them die."

Medical school In 1921, Lin Qiaozhi went with a girl friend to Shanghai to take the entrance examinations for the Xie He ("shi-eh h-e") Medical College of Beijing. The college was run by American missionaries and the college and its hospital are well known in China for their high standards.

It was summer and very hot. When Lin Qiaozhi's friend fainted under the strain and the heat, nobody moved to help her. Lin Qiaozhi stood up immediately and said to the examiner in English: "I will take her out and find her sister, and then I will come back and finish my exam."

She did not manage to finish it, but the examiner was impressed by this determined young woman who showed great compassion for another at her own

A 1990 postage stamp honoring one of China's most dedicated doctors, Lin Qiaozhi.

expense. She was accepted as a student.

In the 1920s it was rare for a woman to be a medical undergraduate. Most women trained as nurses, and when they married, the unwritten rule was that they were dismissed. This was something Lin Qiaozhi understood. By nature she was warm and sociable, but she had her heart set on helping mothers, and for that reason she knew she had to sacrifice her personal life. Later she would say half jokingly, "Could I ever find a man of my generation who would let me carry on with my career the way I wanted?"

At college, Lin Qiaozhi studied for eight hard years and graduated with distinction. She became one of the first women interns and resident doctors at Xie He Hospital. When the chief resident was away for two years on sick leave, she took over his job.

She was sent to the London School of Medicine and the Manchester School of Medicine where she studied gynecology. She also studied at the Chicago Medical College.

Right: Lin Qiaozhi wanted to be a gynecologist because she had lost her mother at an early age, and having experienced a motherless childhood, did not want other children to suffer this fate.

Opposite: Students laying wreaths at the Monument to the People's Heroes in Tiananmen Square during the Qing Ming festival. This was in memory of the late Premier Zhou Enlai and to protest the excesses of the Cultural Revolution. Lin Qiaozhi joined the demonstrators in Tiananmen.

Compassionate doctor In 1941, when the Japanese attacked Pearl Harbor, the hospital was closed, and Lin Qiaozhi set up her own clinic. There was a great shortage of doctors, and many of those who went into private practice made fortunes. But not Lin Qiaozhi, for she never took money from people who could not afford the fee, and sometimes gave her own money to her patients for food and medicine. She became a legend in Beijing. After the surrender of the Japanese, she returned to the Xie He Hospital.

Just before the Communists took over Beijing in 1949, a friend gave Lin Qiaozhi an airplane ticket so she could escape, but she refused it. Lin Qiaozhi continued to work at the Xie He Hospital and was the director of the gynecology department. As a vice-president of the All-China Women's Federation she was able to influence policies for the care and protection of women and children.

She always believed in preventive medicine and was put in charge of organizing the prevention and treatment of cervical cancer in Beijing.

She worked at her profession until

her death in 1982. It is said that her very name had a tranquilizing effect on patients. She was always warm, cheerful, encouraging, and gracious. She cared equally for all patients regardless of rank, power, or wealth. Many people named their babies after her, like Nianlin (Remember Lin), Yanglin (Admire Lin), Jinglin (Respect Lin). Others would write, addressing her as "Mother Lin."

Woman of principle Lin Qiaozhi was also a woman of principle. During the Cultural Revolution she was attacked as a "bourgeois authority" and forced to stop working. At a time when people were afraid to know anyone who was in political trouble, she would still recognize her friends and was not afraid to speak to young friends on the street whose parents had been thrown into prison.

In 1976, wreaths were being laid in Tiananmen Square in memory of the late Premier Zhou Enlai and to protest against the abuses of the Cultural Revolution. Although in her 70s, Lin Qiaozhi went to Tiananmen to be with the people. For a woman of her position, going there at that time bordered on a political crime, and her office was searched as a result.

Until her death, she went on treating patients and teaching new students. She was never lonely as her warm inner spirit was positively infectious. She had many friends and her students loved her.

> "If the motherland has good times, we'll go with her through the good times. If she has bad times, we'll go with her through them too."
> —*Lin Qiaozhi*

Liu Xiaoqing meeting with her fans. She wanted to be an actress from the time she was a child.

Liu Xiaoqing

Liu Xiaoqing ("shi-ao-ching") is one of China's most famous, and perhaps one of the most versatile, film stars. She was born in 1953 in Sichuan province to schoolteachers. When young she was deeply influenced by her father's love for Chinese history and literature.

Childhood dreams Liu Xiaoqing always wanted to be an actress. She wrote this in one of her school compositions when she was nine years old: "My wish is to be an actress, and I wish each of my performances will be met with a bouquet of flowers and thunderous applause." She was roundly criticized for displaying a bourgeois desire for personal fame and gain.

After elementary school, Liu Xiao-qing went to the secondary school affiliated with the Sichuan School of Music in Chengdu. There she was assigned to play the Chinese dulcimer. This disappointed her because she wanted to act.

For the first year, instead of practicing the dulcimer, she read all the books she could from the library. At the year-end concert, she made a fool of herself by not being able to play her solo piece, but being a sensible, strong-minded girl, she spent the next two years practicing hard until she had mastered the dulcimer.

Off to the country Then the Cultural Revolution broke out. She saw her father, whom she loved dearly, beaten, abused, and humiliated. His leg was

Her way

In her autobiography, *My Road*, Liu Xiaoqing wrote:

"After I was made up, I sat in front of a mirror. The film director, the photographers, a whole lot of people crowded around me gesticulating, making critical remarks. Without any scruples they discussed all the faults of my face, my eyes, my chin, my forehead, my mouth. They missed nothing and talked as if I wasn't even there, as though I were a statue to nitpick and probe over. I had no idea that my face had so many faults. All I wanted to do was look for a hole in which to crawl. I ran back to the hostel, covered my head with the quilt and wept.

"After I had finished crying , I sat up. I just couldn't understand it. So what if I was ugly? I never thought I was good looking. You people asked me to come here, what do you mean by throwing mud on my face in front of others? Are all actresses great beauties? Many are not. I was not going to give in. I would do my utmost to act well. So what if I had a prominent forehead. Maybe they'll say after they've seen my performance that it was good that the character had a prominent forehead.

"I ran to the library and borrowed a lot of books. All of Stanislavsky's works. I tried reading them, but could not understand what I read. Then in my room I went over the parts the director had given me to rehearse, eight, nine, ten times each. I used my own intuition to be my most severe critic."

broken and he was refused treatment. The Red Guards demanded she renounce her father and stand on the side of revolution, but she refused. In those days it was a very brave thing to do. She was known as "a dog's bastard," the name given to the children of people in political trouble.

Then at the age of 16, she was sent to the countryside, to a state farm in northern Sichuan. There the first thing she had to do was "win recognition" as a laborer. This she did by working as hard as any of the young men.

Xiaoqing was full of life—she worked in the fields, and at night she caught eels and frogs in the rice fields to "improve the diet." Often, she would sing and play to entertain the other young people, and everybody called her a happy person. She was given an award as an advanced worker of the farm.

Later she joined the People's Liberation Army, first working in the propaganda section, then in the army drama troupe.

Dreams do come true In 1979 she made the film *Xiao Hua*, which was the turning point in her career. She played the part of a simple but courageous village girl. In one of the scenes she is on her knees going uphill on a flight of stone steps, pulling along a wounded soldier. To make it realistic, she practiced every day, crawling up steps until her knees bled. When a copy of the film was shown at the Beijing Film Studio the director was so impressed that he said, "Let's get that actress."

Fame at last In 1980, Liu Xiaoqing acted in *Savage Land*, bringing to life the character of Hua Jinzi, a young countrywoman who is kind and innocent, yet bold and vigorous. This film brought her international fame, although it was not shown widely in China. In 1983 she was invited to play the role of Empress Dowager Ci Xi in two films— *The Burning of Yuan Ming Yuan* and *Behind the Screen*. She played the young Ci Xi ("tse shee"), an intelligent girl of 16 who won the emperor's love, and then the empress dowager, an overwhelming, ruthless, and at times vindictive, woman.

In the film *Hibiscus Town* she plays with charm the part of Hu Yuyin, an ordinary young woman in western Hunan caught in the social upheaval of the Cultural Revolution. In the *Dream of the Red Chamber* she plays the part of Wang Xifeng, the intelligent and capable young matron of the Jia family.

Controversial figure Fame and a career have not come easily to Liu Xiaoqing. She married, but her busy film career took her away from home and her marriage broke up.

Sadly, Chinese society even today is still strongly biased against actresses and many rumors circulated about her films. Stories persisted that there were two versions of *Savage Land*, one for China and another for foreign viewers. In the film allegedly for foreign viewers, she is supposed to have appeared in a nude scene. To the Chinese mind this is the depth of degradation. This was not true, but it was one of the reasons that led to the break-up of her marriage and made her life so difficult at the time. She is now married to Jiang Wen, the actor who played the leading role in the film *Red Sorghum*.

Although Liu Xiaoqing has a natural gift for acting, she has spent many years carefully studying the theory of film acting.

For Liu Xiaoqing art is everything. "I live for my art," she says, "the crucial thing is, under any circumstances to persist in one's beliefs, and never to give in to any difficulty, no matter how great. I worship art, and if necessary would, without hesitation, give everything to it."

Again this attitude is quite opposed to the Communist theory that art exists to serve politics; she is only free to even think, speak or act in this way because this is a period of reform. She remains quite a controversial figure in the Chinese film world.

> **It is hard being a human being. It is hard to be a woman. It's even harder to be a famous woman. And to be a single woman who is famous is exceedingly hard.**
>
> —*Liu Xiaoqing*

Yang Jiang

Yang Jiang is a scholar, playwright, translator, and writer. She was born in Beijing in 1911, the fourth child in a family of eight children. When she was small, she lived in Shanghai, as well as in the two ancient cities of Suzhou and Hangzhou, because of her father's work. Hers was a happy family. Her parents' relationship was one of much love and caring, unlike marriages of the time in which the husband commanded and the wife obeyed.

Yang Jiang's father came into contact with Western democratic thought quite early. He studied first in Japan and later received a master's degree in law in the United States. As a young man he believed in revolution, then after studying in the United States he came to believe in reform.

From an early age Yang Jiang loved to read. When her father was busy she helped by copying case records for him. She did this by hand with a brush, and her calligraphy became excellent. Her father was very exacting, and this taught her accuracy.

At school Yang Jiang was very good at mathematics and science, but when it came to choosing a career, she knew she loved literature. Her father advised her, "Whatever you love best is closest to your character and the most fitting thing to study." So she studied literature at Qinghua University in Beijing.

At Qinghua University, she met

Yang Jiang, writer.

Qian Zhongshu ("chee-en jhohng-shu"), another student of literature, whom she married in 1935. Like her parents' marriage, theirs was one of love and deep friendship. Qian Zhongshu was to become one of the foremost Chinese novelists of the 20th century.

After their marriage they went to Oxford where Qian Zhongshu studied literature. After Oxford, they went to Paris for a year where Yang Jiang continued her studies of French literature and Qian audited courses.

The Cleansing Bath, left, and Just Before I Drink the Tea, two of Yang Jiang's latest works.

were popular and well received.

In 1949 when the Communists came to power, Qian Zhongshu was offered a job at Oxford. He refused, however, and remained in China. Yang Jiang was assigned to work in the Chinese Academy of Social Sciences. In 1958 she began studying Spanish on her own. Just before the Cultural Revolution, she worked on a Chinese translation of *Don Quixote*. During the Cultural Revolution, the Red Guards took the text from her and threw it in a rubbish heap. She managed to retrieve it and completed the translation after the Cultural Revolution. It was published in 1978 and is now in its fifth printing. For this work she received an award from the Spanish government.

During the Cultural Revolution she was seized by the Red Guards and humiliated. Then she was forced to go to the May Seventh Cadre School. Upon returning to Beijing, she wrote *Six Chapters of Life in a Cadre School*, which tells of how she lived and what she did there. She has since written two other books, *Just Before I Drink the Tea* and *The Cleansing Bath*. *Just Before I Drink the Tea* tells of her life both before and after 1949, including the period of the Cultural Revolution. *The Cleansing Bath* is a novel about Chinese intellectuals. Yang Jiang's wit and irony are both sharp and penetrating and her language is simple and vivid, yet stylish.

Yang Jiang is not a Communist and

Return to China Back in China in the summer of 1938, Yang Jiang stayed in Shanghai to care for her father and mother-in-law, her own mother having died a little earlier. Her husband joined the Southwest Associated University, which was made up of the three major universities of northern China—Beijing, Qinghua and Nankai—that had amalgamated and moved south because of the Japanese invasion. In late 1941, Qian returned to Shanghai to attend to his very ill father-in-law. He, Yang Jiang and their families were trapped there by the outbreak of the Pacific War.

Yang Jiang and Qian Zhongshu lived in the French concession of Shanghai. Qian managed to secure an appointment at the French Catholic Aurora Women's College. At the same time, Yang Jiang was writing plays that were successfully produced as part of the "theater boom" in war-time Shanghai. Her plays *As You Desire*, *Swindle* and *Sport of the World*

Dare to say no

Towards some things my father was quite strict. I was 16 and studying in senior high school. At the time...there were a lot of activities in the student movement, demonstrations, mass meetings and so on. Once the Student's Union asked each school to do publicity in the streets—which involved standing on a bench and speaking to passers-by. It was suggested I take part in this publicity. I was 16 at the time, but I looked 14, and when I became anxious I would blush....

At the weekend when I went home, I went to my father to ask him to come to the rescue. I asked him if I could say "My family didn't approve." He replied with a no. He said, "If you don't want to go, then don't go. Don't use your father as an excuse." I said, "It won't work, the minority has to submit to the majority."

"If you should submit to them, then do so," he said. "If you have reasons, you can explain them. Whether you go or not, it's up to you."

But my reason was the sort of thing that was hard to explain. How could I say my skin was thinner than others?

Father then told me of a funny thing about himself. When he was judge at the High Court of Jiangsu, a warlord by the name of Cheng Dechuan arrived in Shanghai. The local gentry put an ad in the newspaper with their names in it welcoming him. My father found his name was on the list without having been consulted. Father did not welcome this warlord....So my father put an ad in the paper in big characters stating he was not part of welcome party.

"You know what Lincoln said: Dare to say no!" he added. "Do you dare?"

Troubled, I replied "I do." Unfortunately it wasn't for a great cause. Just the fact that a shy girl didn't want to make a fool of herself. I returned to school still without a good excuse. All I insisted on was "I don't agree, I'm not going!"

(An extract from *Just Before I Drink the Tea*, Yang Jiang)

coming from the old society she brought with her the liberal and humanist values her father and family had given her. There is none of the artificiality and boring bombastic lecturing so prevalent in the modern Chinese writing of mainland China. She has also written academic papers on literature, translation, and the novel.

Yang Jiang lives very privately with her husband. Now that she has been acclaimed internationally, the relevant Communist bureaucrats have decided to recognize her too. However, she and her husband both refuse the accolades the authorities want to bestow upon them. "I've lived all my life unknown and without position," she says, "it's been very free." She also says with humor, "We're both like very old mahogany furniture. If you move us about too much, we'll fall apart."

Yang Jiang writes for herself, not for the politics of the day. Her detachment permits this, something very difficult for a writer to do in mainland China today. Reading her works is like looking at a bamboo grove: it is clean, upright, green and forthright, and always there—a real part of China.

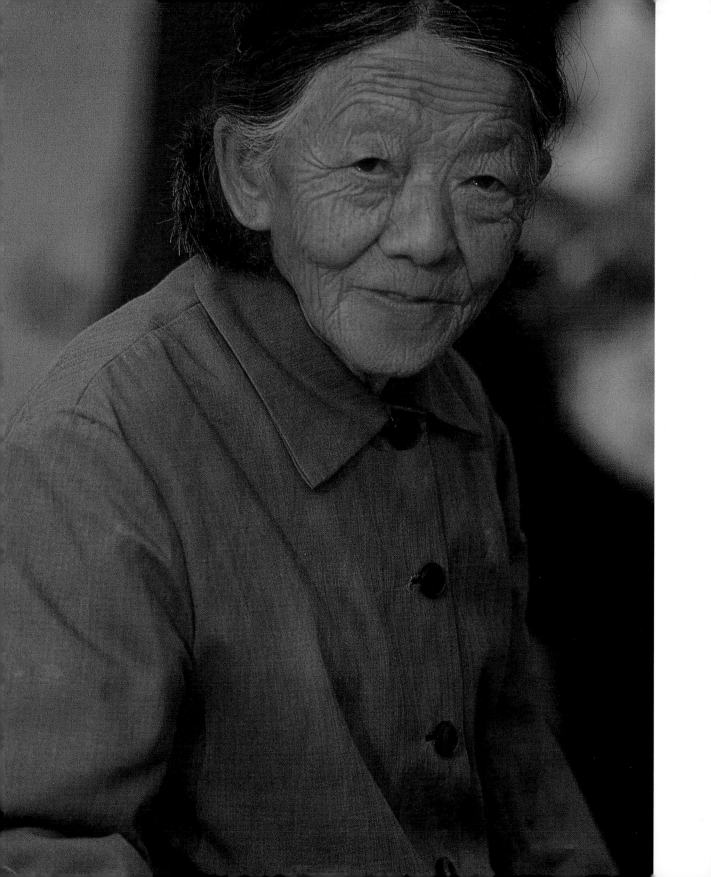

chapter six

A Lifetime

he Chinese woman's life has been ruled by men from cradle to grave; she had to obey her father when young, obey her husband after marriage, and obey her son when old. But the Chinese woman of today is slowly coming into her own. While the man is still dominant, she is beginning to assert herself. She no longer obeys her father unquestioningly, particularly when it comes to marriage. With some economic independence, she no longer suffers a bad husband passively; she fights back, sometimes with the help of the law. In old age, she is not necessarily dependent on her son and can therefore choose to live apart from him and his family. In this chapter we look at the life stages of the Chinese woman of today.

Birth and the girl child

In the old days, the birth of a boy was always heralded with great joy, the birth of a girl not necessarily so. Female infanticide has been a custom over the centuries, particularly in poor areas if many girls were born to a family. The birth of a boy meant a guarantee for the parents in old age, as sons were expected to take care of their parents. A daughter was like a "guest" in the house, for as soon as she reached marrying age, she went to live in someone else's home. Today, while there are families who welcome the birth of a daughter, the prevailing attitude in Chinese society is preference for a son.

The tranquility of age (*opposite*) and impish youth (*right*). The Chinese woman of today is beginning to assert herself.

Resting the month

The birth of a child is a very special time for Han Chinese women. For according to tradition, a woman has the right to rest for the first month after giving birth. It is called *zuo yuezi* ("joo-ore you-eh-je") or, "resting the month." On the whole this is strictly adhered to, even today. Western-trained doctors insist there is no medical reason to justify this. Some say Chinese women themselves institutionalized it, as it was the only way they could ever get a decent rest. Whatever the reason, it has remained the custom.

During the period of the *yuezi*, there are many taboos. The new mother must not place her hands in cold water. Some say she must not read as it will affect her eyesight. She must not expose her body to any cold air. Any pains or aches that result during this period will remain lifetime ailments. So, even in summer, the nursing mother for the first month must be covered from head to toe.

Only certain foods may be eaten, to help produce milk and keep the body warm. These foods include millet, which has plenty of vitamin B, ginger-fried meats, meat and fish soups for bringing on the mother's milk, tofu, fresh vegetables, and so on.

Very often the mother or mother-in-law will wait on the new mother, cooking, cleaning and washing for her. In cities, if a relative is not available, a maid is engaged for that month to wait on the mother and the newborn baby. In the countryside the husband will cook and care for his wife, particularly if the couple are very poor and have no one in the family to help them. In such circumstances, the new mother cannot rest for a whole month. Often she can only rest for 12 to 15 days, after which she is back on her feet.

A walk in the park. While some welcome the birth of a girl, most Chinese still prefer boys over girls.

There are husbands and parents-in-law who abuse and mistreat a daughter-in-law who has given birth to a daughter. The government has imposed legal sanctions against such mistreatment. However, custom is strong and in many places the daughter-in-law often has to put up with this poor treatment. However, there are husbands who love and support their wives and who disagree with their parents' attitudes. In such circumstances, having a daughter is less difficult and more bearable for the wife.

In the past, girls were often named after flowers or other plants. A girl born in December might be named Shuemei

(Snow Plum), one born in April might be named Chunhua (Spring Blossom). There were also many poetic names like Zhixia (Weaver of the Sunset) or names indicating character, such as Shumin (Kind and Sensitive). After 1949 political names became fashionable. Names like Aijun (Loves the Army), Jin (Progress) or simply Hong meaning "red," were popular. Today people no longer pick political names.

Country babies

In rural areas boys are still preferred to girls. For the young mother who has given birth to a boy, there is much pride and relief. For the rest of the family, this is a moment of great joy.

In many parts of rural China the celebration of the birth of a son is quite grand. When the baby boy is 20 days old, the family celebrates his birth and growth. The baby is given an amulet or a necklace with a silver locket he will wear until the age of 12. The maternal grandmother gives him the most gifts. These include clothing she has made from remnants of cloth taken from many families. This is called *baijiayi*—clothing from 100 families—and symbolizes the blessings of 100 families. The maternal grandmother also takes a lot of nourishing food to her daughter.

At this celebration, the baby is also named. At weddings, fun is made of the bride. At the "20th day" celebration, the villagers make fun of the paternal

grandparents. They smear the grandmother's face with black soot to indicate jubilation, and parade the grandfather on an ox to show the happiness of a growing family.

When the boy is one month old, the mother returns to her parents' home for 10 days. The purpose of the move is to change the baby's surroundings and introduce it to outside life. When the mother leaves her parents' home, the maternal grandmother will bake several cakes, as a token of blessing to her grandchild. These will later be given to the other village children so they may share the blessings.

Generally, when a girl is one month old her hair and eyebrows are shaved in the belief that they will grow back thick and dark. But there is no formal celebration to herald the birth of a girl.

Looking out the window. In the country, baby boys are luckier than girls. Their birth is celebrated with great fanfare, with lots of gifts from relatives. Girls only have their hair and eyebrows shaved so they will grow back dark and thick.

> If parents behave well, children follow their example without being told; if parents behave poorly, children refuse to be disciplined.
>
> —*Confucius*

Bringing up the only child

In the cities, with the one-child family planning policy, a daughter can become very spoiled, not to mention a son. From the time she is a baby, she is doted upon and waited on by six adults—four grandparents and two parents. Women who are now retired feel they have to make up for the time and love they could not give their own children, and they do this by spoiling their grandchild.

Girls have become known as "little princesses." Boys are called "little emperors." Many children from one-child families are willful, individualistic,

Grandparents and their young charge. Children from one-child families are greatly fussed-over by grandparents and parents.

selfish, and self-centered, and this creates problems for their integration into school and society.

These are problems that are now being recognized. Starting in 1989, the *Chinese Women's Newspaper* has run articles on subjects such as "How to be a Good Parent" and "How to be a Good Mother."

However, the problem persists because of the way Chinese women bring up their sons. Most Chinese mothers and grandmothers wait on their sons as though they were kings. They will not teach them to be considerate and thoughtful toward their mothers and women in general. While some mothers correct their daughter's behavior, they will not necessarily do the same with their sons. Daughters are taught to help their mothers; sons are rarely taught to do so. If the father does not do household chores, the son won't either. Perhaps the answer to the question of equality lies with women, who must first of all change the attitude of their sons toward women.

City girls

The majority of babies are cared for by neighbors, relatives or friends, for which the parents will pay a fee. Sometimes the baby is looked after by grandparents or a maid. Some factories, institutes, and central government agencies have day care centers, and mothers have nursing time off.

At the age of four, many city children go to a nursery. They begin school at the age of seven and a half or eight. After-school care is sometimes organized by the neighborhood committee for working parents. However, many children have the house key tied around their necks, so they can go home by themselves. For small children this is hardly satisfactory.

At school both boys and girls receive the same education and treatment. Often it is the girls who study well and first join the Young Pioneers League, which is a children's organization of the Communist Party that trains children in the values and discipline the Communists want. All members wear a red scarf. This is very important, and all parents encourage their children to join the organization. Parents see this as a sign that their child has been socially accepted.

Adolescence The adolescence of an urban Chinese girl is basically centered around her studies. In many lower-income families, girls have to help their mothers; when very young they learn how to make steamed bread and help with the laundry, shopping, and cleaning.

In most families, studying is considered as important for girls as for boys. To study well is part of traditional Chinese culture, and gaining entry into the university opens a doorway into the government bureaucracy, thus providing a secure job for life. This is the goal many Chinese parents have for their children because they themselves were deprived of education during the Cultural Revolution.

Parents spur their children on, hoping they will have a bright future and not have to spend all their life in some menial job with low pay and low social status.

Home from the market. Girls in the city are taught to help with household chores from a young age. But their lives as adolescents revolve around their schoolwork, in preparation for the all-important college entrance examiniations.

Many parents buy pianos and violins and make their children learn to play them, with no regard for the children's interests. They demand that teachers assign more homework and press their children to memorize poetry or mathematical formulas. Often the result is children have little time or energy for sports, rest, or recreation. Often too, the pressure results in a wide generation gap between parents and children. It also creates unrealistic expectations for many children.

Education for parents

One primary school in Beijing set up an adult education center for parents in 1984. It has been eagerly attended since the moment it went into operation. The center invites specialists to lecture parents on child psychology and other problems.

In a lecture to parents, Zhao Zhongxin of the Scientific Education Research Institute at Beijing Normal University stressed that they should respect the child's personality, encourage creativity, and promote honesty and a willingness to admit mistakes. Most of the audience agreed, but some argued that an adult so open would get nowhere in Chinese society today. Most government officials, they said, received promotion because they quietly followed orders; anyone who dared to disagree with superiors got into trouble. A child raised according to Zhao's ideas would run into a brick wall as soon as he grew up and got a job. Such are the contradictions of the society.

Surveys of parents reveal that the overwhelming majority wish their children to become skilled in a profession. Not even 1% wanted their children to train for professional sports careers.

A recent primary school survey also revealed that 5% of children saw themselves becoming factory workers, and only 1% farmers. The reality of Chinese society, however, says otherwise.

Today, with the economic reforms, new avenues are opening up for girls. Careers in modelling, acting, dress designing, art, and business formerly considered not socially respectable are now acceptable. Women make good money in these fields.

Girls in rural areas

In rural China most girls do not go to school or study like their city counterparts. As we have seen in Chapter 4, a girl in rural China is at a distinct disadvantage because, even when very young, she is considered part of the family's labor force and is not given time to study. In this sense she and her city sister are worlds apart.

Education Illiteracy remains high in rural areas. There is a high drop-out rate in rural schools, because rural children must help in earning money.

There are a number of children who cannot go to school because their parents cannot afford the fees. Education is not free in rural areas. Fees vary from region to region. In more prosperous regions, the local government might pay the fees for students who cannot afford them. In most areas, however, the local government itself does not have sufficient funding. When a choice has to be made about who will go to school, it is always the boy who will go; the girl stays home to work.

Country girls complete an average of three to five years of school. Forty years have passed since China was supposed to have moved from the old society into the new one, but in rural areas, it has done little to eliminate the traditional male bias against girls to give women an education.

With the economic reforms, there has been a virtual return to family farming and production. Thus the value of family labor is high, and this has given parents the impetus to keep their children, particularly their daughters, out of school.

In Fujian province, in the fishing villages, daughters make and mend nets, otherwise the family will have to hire someone to do it. Girls as young as eight can catch prawns at low tide and earn $1.40 or $1.60 for three or four hours of work. So why send them to school? Many girls work in rural village enterprises, knitting, embroidering, sewing, or making handicrafts, earning about $20 a month. Girls in full-time schools often drop out to do this kind of work and help increase the family income.

To solve this problem the Fujian Provincial Educational Committee has instituted night school classes for girls. The aim is to widen the reach of full-time schools and eventually make them universal. In the meantime, the night school runs three-year courses. Pupils attend school five nights a week, two hours per session. They learn 1,000 Chinese words, which takes them to the threshold of literacy. (The literacy level is 1,250 words.) They also learn basic arithmetic.

Before the school term begins, teachers in the various counties go from door to door persuading parents to send their daughters to school. They still meet parents who say, "What's the good of girls going to school? They just get married into other families when they grow up."

However, it has also been found that as people become successful in their family businesses, they see all too well the disadvantages of a lack of education, particularly since many such people had

Working on the farm. When a choice has to be made about who will go to school, the boys usually get to go, while the girls have to stay home and work.

very little schooling during the Cultural Revolution (1966–1976). They have come to understand that modern business requires educated workers, and some are thus beginning to send their daughters to school willingly.

Factory girls outside their dormitories. Single girls do not get rooms to themselves, only married couples do. They share rooms in dormitories instead.

The single woman

Remaining a single woman in China today is not an easy choice, even in the big cities. In the countryside, it is almost impossible. The social pressures are too great because Chinese consider being single abnormal. Women who choose to remain unmarried are on the whole well educated, professsionals, or else are young and wish to continue their studies.

There are many difficulties for single women. They must continue living at home because housing is scarce and the work unit very rarely allots a room to a single worker. A single woman may, however, stay in the dormitory of her workplace and return home on weekends.

At home she is subjected to pressures from the family, relatives, neighbors and friends, all "concerned" about her not marrying. At work she is subjected to many pressures, including those from well-meaning colleagues who insist on introducing her to a likely partner. Sometimes her life can be made miserable by nasty gossip about her single status.

If her parents are understanding, it is easier for a girl to withstand the pressure. If, however, the parents insist on her marrying, then life for her is doubly difficult.

Single women are very rare in the countryside, and it is only women who have some very obvious physical or mental disability who do not marry.

Government matchmaking centers

In the early '80s the women's federation, the Communist youth league, the trade unions and the local government set up matchmaking centers in many cities. This was because of the large number of single people age 28 and older.

A 1984 survey revealed that there were 150,000 single people in Beijing who were over 28 years of age, and 160,000 in Shanghai. Most of these young people had been sent to the remote countryside to work during the Cultural Revolution, and on returning many had entered the university. In China university students are not permitted to marry, and on graduation, these young people found it difficult to find a partner. The government thus decided to help.

Courtship and marriage

For a girl it is very important to be married. It is part of the social norm, and it is considered a misfortune not to be married. The Marriage Law stipulates a girl may only be married when she reaches the age of 23. In rural areas, this is considered late. In the cities, many girls marry much later than 23.

In Chinese cities today, most young people are still brought together in the traditional way—by a matchmaker. Nowadays the matchmaker only acts as a bridge, while the final decision is made by the young people themselves. This kind of voluntary marriage accounts for a large proportion of modern marriages.

Matchmakers are no longer professional in the old sense. A friend, a parent, or a relative can act as matchmaker. Generally they are given a present as a token of thanks if the marriage match works out.

Marriage is a lifelong partnership and many considerations have to be taken into account in choosing a spouse in China. Age is important, as are career, educational background—a criterion most educated women look at—in-laws, social status and, very important, political background. For instance, if a girl comes from a family that has been politically persecuted, there are young men who will not marry her for fear of jeopardizing their own careers or of becoming vulnerable to future political persecution.

At the disco. Even in the cities, couples are brought together by matchmakers, who may be relatives, friends, or colleagues.

Educated women find it hard to get married

Many Chinese men want to choose as their partners women who are not as highly educated as themselves. They want women who are prepared to give time and energy to the family and home and who will support their career. They do not want a wife competing with them. As a consequence well-educated young women or young women who wish to further their studies and pursue a career have difficulty finding a husband.

There are strong-willed young women who refuse to get married unless they can find someone after their own heart. That takes courage. But there are understanding parents who wish for their daughter's happiness and who do not exert pressure on them to marry early.

Engagement There are no formal celebrations for an engagement. There is an exchange of presents between the families of the couple, and the parents of the young man will visit the girl's home where they have lunch or dinner.

Once a couple is engaged, it is difficult to break the engagement, particularly on the part of the girl. That one does not love the man is not an easily accepted excuse, particularly if both families have already agreed to the marriage.

Today, even in the cities there are young women who do not wish to go through with their marriage but feel obliged to do so because the social pressures are too great to ignore.

Marriage in the rural areas In the countryside marriage arranged by parents and matchmakers is still a widespread practice. Generally matchmakers will introduce a young couple to each other.

After the introduction, the young people may be allowed to make up their own minds. But often parents have the final say in the match.

Expensive betrothal presents are given by the man's family to the woman's once both families agree to the match.

Sometimes a rebellious girl will run away from an arranged marriage and seek help from sympathetic city people. The legal authorities will help her, but this is a very costly and time-consuming business. An investigation has to be made. Then the authorities have to go to the village to explain the law to her parents and to the bridegroom and his parents. They are warned they have violated the Marriage Law. When all parties finally agree to dissolve the match, presents including gifts of money have to be returned. Both families will feel they have lost face.

Tradition and custom are strong and most girls go through with the arranged marriage without a fight.

Wedding ceremony

The wedding ceremony in today's urban China among the Han Chinese is a very simple affair. Both the man and the woman must first obtain a letter from his or her place of work stating marital status, sex, date of birth, ethnic group, and the identity of the intended spouse. It should also indicate whether there are any close blood ties between the two. In the case of unemployed or self-employed persons, the letter may come from their neighborhood committee. This document is valid for one month from its date of issue.

The pair take these letters to the local marriage registration office and fill in an application form. They must also bring along proof of residence, medical certificates, and three copies of a photograph of them together. Divorced persons should produce their divorce certificates.

The couple are each given a marriage certificate. A copy of the photograph is pasted on, and the certificate is stamped

and signed. With this simple registration procedure the two are legally married.

Before the 1980s, the couple would return to their home to a celebration party with friends and workmates. According to custom, sweets of "happiness" were given to friends, colleagues, and acquaintances.

These simple celebrations were considered the revolutionary way to do things. When people were not very well off, it certainly was practical.

A country wedding. Arranged marriages are still prevalent in the country, and it is very difficult for a girl to break off a match.

Wedding customs in the country

The rural south

In the provinces of Zhejiang and Jiangsu where there are many rivers, the bride goes to her wedding in a boat. Several boats transport the dowry, a band of musicians, the bridal attendants, and the guests. Following tradition the bride sits on a bamboo chair holding two small "treasure heaters," charcoal heaters on which people heat their feet. She is carried to her boat by four young men. The custom symbolizes the hope that the bride will bear descendants and bring happiness to her husband's family.

Among silkworm breeders

When a girl gets married in a village of silkworm breeders, she pins a cocoon in her hair and has among her dowry silk clothes, silk quilt covers, and silk fabric. Her dowry also includes two mulberry saplings, silkworm eggs, and baskets. Apart from wishing luck to the bride and the groom, wedding guests also wish them a good harvest of silk. In the first year of her marriage, the new bride is expected to raise a certain number of silkworms by herself to prove her skill to her in-laws.

The rural north

In the old days a sedan chair borne by carriers took the bride from her home to her husband's home. In the 1950s the bride went on horseback. In the 1960s she went on a bicycle; in the 1970s by tractor. Now she goes by car. Marriages generally take place during festivals or holidays. When the weather is cold the bride wears a high-necked satin brocade jacket of padded silk that is both warm and pretty.

Friends and relatives gather at the home of the bridegroom's parents and there is a banquet. At night everyone goes to the bridal chamber and teases the bride. There is food and wine. Firecrackers are set off and the couple made to eat an apple attached to a string and dangled by someone standing on a table.

If they can afford it, the young people may build their own home before the marriage. However, they often live with the husband's parents. After marriage, the young wife is expected to work with the family and be helpful to her in-laws. The birth of a son immediately makes her a good daughter-in-law in the eyes of her husband's family.

New ways of celebrating With the new prosperity of the 1980s and the 1990s, weddings have become more elaborate. Many girls today wear white bridal gowns and veils, and receptions are held similar to those in the West. City brides very rarely wear the traditional red silk gown that Chinese brides used to wear, although red traditionally signifies happiness.

Wedding receptions are sometimes held in big hotels. Often several couples will hold their receptions together. The government encourages this in order to cut ostentation and extravagance. It has its practical side, as it is less costly, and there are more people and more fun.

At the reception the marriage certificates are read. Then, according to Chinese custom, the bridegroom crosses arms with his bride to drink a cup of wine. The couple bow to the guests and to their parents. Then they bow to each other three times. The first bow signifies the love between husband and wife; the second signifies mutual steadfastness; the third bow signifies having a healthy baby.

A wedding in Beijing. In a compromise with custom, the bride wears a red suit instead of the traditional red silk gown. She carries a bouquet, which is a borrowed Western custom.

Father taking his daughter to the nursery in his bicycle basket. Young men today are more willing to share household chores with their wives, some even doing the cooking if the wife is working late.

Motherhood and the family

In the city In the Chinese society of today, the emphasis is on making money and improving one's standard of living, to provide the family with the comforts of modern life such as a gas stove, a refrigerator, a washing machine, a television, and a video recorder. For a young mother modern appliances are important as they lighten her burden. In the cities today, many live in nuclear families, consisting of parents and children. Unlike in the past, there are no grandparents to help with the housekeeping.

Before going to work early in the morning, the child must be awakened, fed, dressed, and dropped off at the nursery school. Very often it is the mother who does this, although there are fathers who take the child to the nursery or to school.

The main means of transportation in both urban and rural China are the bicycle and the bus. A little seat for the child is secured at the front or the back of the bicycle. Many cities and towns forbid elementary school children to ride bicycles, so parents have to take the child to school on their bicycles.

After delivering the child at the nursery or elementary school, the mother cycles off to work. In smaller cities or towns where peasants bring fresh poultry, fish, and vegetables to town in the early morning, the mother might go first to the market to shop for the day's food, which she takes with her to work. At lunch time she goes home to cook the midday meal. The family will all go home to lunch. In southern China where it is very hot, the lunch break is three hours in summer and one and a half hours in winter.

In big cities like Beijing, where the population is 10 million, most people take their lunch to work or eat in the company canteen. Lunch breaks are shorter, one hour in the winter and two hours in summer. Employees in factories and shops have even shorter lunch breaks, generally only half an hour.

After another four hours of work—China has a 48-hour work week—the child is collected. In a big city like Beijing or Shanghai, the mother might do some shopping on the way home and then return to cook the evening meal. Today among younger Chinese, many men will help their wives with the cooking.

As many families now have washing machines, washing is done at the end of the week rather than daily. But during the week there are other chores to be done like cleaning and mending. Families watch television in the evenings. But some families do not watch television at all so that the child can concentrate on his or her homework.

Schools in China give children a lot of homework that the parents are expected to supervise; parents are required to sign the child's homework. Every night, except on Sundays, until about nine o'clock, a mother will spend time with her child helping him or her do the homework. Even during school holidays, elementary school children are required to do at least two hours of homework a day.

Parents want their child to join the Young Pioneers League, the Communist children's organization. To do so, the child must obtain high marks in mathematics and Chinese. This adds to the pressure faced by parents and children.

The mother usually fits in housework with the supervision of the child's homework. So while a child is doing arithmetic or calligraphy, the mother will be sweeping the floor or dusting the furniture, or taking out the winter clothes and quilts to be aired or putting them away. At the same time she will be watching the child and shouting at him or her every so often: "Are you concentrating?"

On weekends, the family may visit a park or go to a movie or even a concert. Often, however, parents are exhausted after a long, tiring week and prefer to sleep or rest at home. On the whole there is little time for recreation or even personal development.

Waiting for school to be over, but not wasting time. For a mother who works outside the home, every minute is precious.

In rural areas In rural China survival has always been the pivot round which life revolves. Thus for a rural mother the most important task each day is the tending of her sheep, fish, pigs, or whatever is the main source of subsistence.

Children walk to the village school themselves, and they are not as closely supervised as their urban counterparts. Thus, rural children become independent at an earlier age than city children.

Child care is organized during busy seasons, that is when the planting and harvesting seasons are upon them. At other times, the child is cared for by his or her mother or grandmother.

The rural mother of today either

The rural woman's life is harder than the city woman's. Work on the farm is strenuous. At home there are no modern conveniences to make household chores easier. Cooking (*above*) is done on a stove that uses firewood that must be chopped, and washing has to be done by hand in the river (*opposite*).

The Daughter's Festival

The Daughter's Festival is held in Guangyuan, in northern Sichuan on September 1. Guangyuan is the birthplace of Wu Zetian, the only empress in Chinese history whose 50-year rule laid the foundation for the splendid Tang dynasty. Since Wu Zetian became empress in the late 7th century, women in Guangyuan have celebrated the Daughter's Festival every year on Wu Zetian's birthday. After 1949 this was stopped. It has only been revived recently.

This is the only day that women in Guangyuan are free from taking care of the children, cooking meals, feeding pigs, and other work.

On this day women go in groups to the Huangze Temple to worship Wu Zetian. After paying their respects to her, they move to the banks of the Jialing River where they entertain themselves.

Singing is an important activity at this festival. People who are good at singing row fishing boats to Guangyuan from far and near. They compete from the two banks of the river, or from their boats, filling the area with songs about labor, love, hardships, and their worries in life. Some of the songs have been sung for generations while others are impromptu.

works in the fields or the rural factory, or she may even have her own small enterprise such as breeding pigs, fish, or poultry.

Life is hard in the rural areas as the woman does not have any of the conveniences of urban living. She has to fetch water from the well, wash clothes by hand, grind the flour or corn, water the vegetables in the family kitchen garden, and so on.

If there is a television, the family will watch it together. But for the majority of rural people, it is still the custom to sleep when night falls and rise with the sun. Life is still very simple for the majority of women living in the vast rural lands of China.

A woman accountant. Women in China, particularly the educated, are beginning to stand up for their rights.

Protection of women's rights

In a country like China where male domination remains strong, the protection of women's rights is important. In the big urban centers problems exist, but the means to solve them are more available and social attitudes more enlightened. In the vast rural areas, protection of women's rights is a very real issue.

In this respect the women's federation in the counties and townships can often play an important role. Women come to the women's federation to ask for help with problems such as an unwanted arranged marriage, the closing down of nurseries, and mistreatment of wives who give birth to daughters. The problems demand investigation and much work to see that the laws are enforced.

Another body that helps protect women's rights is the people's mediation committee. These committees were set up in 1954 and work under the Ministry of Justice. Their main work is to settle civil disputes by observing legal provisions. They are very important in the Chinese countryside. Between 1981 and 1988 they handled eight times the number of civil cases dealt with by the people's courts in that period. There are more than 3 million mediators throughout the country. In the countryside particularly, they play a positive role in protecting the rights of women and children and in educating the people on the law and the principles and ideas behind the law.

The government has also set up legal aid advisory centers in county towns, townships, and the suburbs. Women can go there for legal advice. The men and women who work in these centers are

> Most divorce suits are initiated by women, something unheard of traditionally....Divorce is one means of safeguarding the dignity of women and freeing them from bullying and humiliation. In this respect it is a sign of progress in the fight for women's liberation...
> —*Lei Jieqiong, President of the Society for Research and Marriage and the Family*

not all lawyers, but they have had some training in the law and are able to give legal advice and mediate family disputes. These centers are proving extremely helpful and useful to women.

Not long ago a group of young women in Anhui, who had gone to school together, wrote a joint letter to a local newspaper complaining of the mistreatment they had received upon giving birth to daughters. This shows that once educated and familiar with their rights, women can stand up for themselves.

Article 16 of the Marriage Law of 1980 states: Children may adopt either their father's or their mother's family name.
Article 11 of the Marriage Law issued in 1950 provides that husband and wife have the right to use either his or her own family name.
Since then it has been the custom in China for women not to take their husband's name, but to continue using their own family name.

All-China Women's Federation

The official women's mass organization, the All-China Women's Federation, was established in 1949, and its work is directed by the Chinese Communist Party. Headquartered in Beijing, the federation has a total of 89,000 women workers across the country.

Through its affiliated organizations at grassroots level, the women's federation does a great deal of work among ordinary women, particularly in rural areas. In early 1989 it launched the Learning and Competing Program. This work is done in cooperation with the Ministry of Agriculture, the Ministry of Forestry, and the State Science and Technological Commission. It encourages women to learn culture (that is, obtain literacy and general education) and technology. Women are also encouraged to compete through personal achievements and making a contribution to society. So far about 120 million women have participated in the program.

The technology taught is simple and practical and has resulted in women increasing production of grain, cotton, and oils. They have also improved quality in silkworm breeding, goose and duck breeding, vegetable and fruit growing, and forestry.

Anti-illiteracy campaigns are also carried out among women all over the country.

The social aim of this program is to help women move away from being dependent to being independent, from being subordinate to taking control of their lives.

Growing old

China has more aged people than any other nation—100 million or 10% of the population. It is estimated that by the middle of next century, China will have approximately 390 million aged people.

Twenty million Chinese over the age of 60 live in cities. The majority of them have a pension, about 70% of their former wages, to live on. The remaining 80 million live in the rural areas; for them there is no state pension and they must depend on their children.

Generally, women live longer than men. According to the 1982 census, 70.6% of China's 35 million senior citizens who lived alone were widows.

In 1983, the All-China Committee on Problems of the Aged was set up. There are local committees in every province and large municipality. The committee ensures health care for old people and protects their rights.

In addition such institutions as the Society for the Aged and the Fund for the Aged have been established.

Life after retirement Women retire at the age of 55 in China. Professional women such as doctors, accountants, and teachers who remain in good health often continue to work after retirement. Some work part-time, others full-time but on contract, receiving both their pension and their salary.

There are those who, on retirement, have set up their own clinic or business. In the city of Hangzhou 18 retired medical personnel, half of whom are women, have set up a counseling service specializing in maternity and child care.

More attention is being paid to recreation for retirees. In the main parks there are classes for *taijiquan* and *qigong*—traditional forms of exercise— and even disco and ballroom dancing is offered. These are always well attended as they are popular, and they add to the social lives of older people.

For many women, retirement is a time to stay at home and perhaps look after the grandchildren. But the women who reach their mid-50s in the 1990s are no longer like Chinese women of the past. They have gone out to work all their lives and mixed freely with friends and colleagues, and the majority

are in good health, so staying at home is something many find hard to adapt to.

For these women, very often the period of adjustment can be quite painful. Some ask to work for the local neighborhood committee. Others have banded together to help organize child care centers in the neighborhood. Some join knitting factories, hand-knitting garments for the export market.

With a working life behind them, many older women also find it difficult to settle down with their children and grandchildren. Living with a daughter-in-law does not necessarily make a mother feel free or relaxed. As one woman said, "Never criticize your daughter-in-law otherwise there will always be some discomfort between the two of you and that's for half a lifetime!"

So rather than risk the strain of such a relationship, and for the sake of peace, some older couples, and especially widows, prefer to find a place to live by themselves. Often this works out reasonably well, with the grandchildren coming over for a meal or for tutoring.

Rural grandmothers In rural areas older people are glad to see their children move out, releasing the parents from heavy household burdens and ensuring them a quiet life. Parents and their married children continue to live in the same courtyard or in houses nearby. To many, breaking up the extended family means only cooking their meals and washing clothes separately; in daily life, sons still listen to their parents, family members help each other, sons are responsible for heavy household chores, and grandparents take care of grandchildren.

Attending calligraphy class with her grandson. Life after retirement can be enriching as there is now time to learn things, which the busy days of work and caring for family do not allow.

Women Firsts

Ban Zhao	First woman historian of China who lived during the Han dynasty (206 B.C.–A.D. 220). In her book *Precepts for Women*, she set down the way women should behave as women, as mothers, and as wives, according to Confucian principles. These rules still influence many Chinese women today.
Dai Ailian	(b. 1883) Pioneer who introduced ballet to China in 1941. Born in Trinidad, she studied ballet in London. In China, she trained dancers and performed, innovatively combining ballet with traditional Chinese dance.
Deng Chunlan	(b. 1896) First woman to campaign for the admission of women into universities. She became one of the first women students at Beijing University in 1920.
He Bo	(b. 1913) The first postwoman in China. In early 1927 she took the oral and written examination at the Hunan Post Office. Out of 500 candidates, she was placed second. She began her job on April 18, 1927, and in May received her first salary, which was 21 silver dollars.
Lian Liru	(b. 1942) First woman to become a professional storyteller, in northern China. Storytelling was a popular art form in China. People paid to listen to storytellers perform stories from legend and history. Now storytellers appear on television and as part of variety shows. Traditionally storytellers were men. Lian's father was one of the best storytellers in the country, and she learned the art from him. She first performed in 1960 at the age of 18.
Li Qingzhao	China's greatest woman poet and the first to write the *ci*, poetry written to a tune, she lived during the Song dynasty (960–1279). Her poetry is still read and appreciated today.
Lu Li	A gymnast, she obtained the first-ever perfect score for the uneven bars, at the 1992 Olympic Games in Barcelona, Spain.
Wu Zetian	(years of reign: A.D. 690–705) China's first and only empress to rule directly from the imperial throne. She introduced many reforms. Although she engaged in war with Korea, the country was at peace internally. Her reign paved the way for the golden age of the Tang dynasty.
Zhang Huilan	(b. 1898) Professor at Shanghai College of Physical Culture. In 1987, at the age of 90, she became the first Chinese to receive the UNESCO award for outstanding contribution in the field of athletics. She was one of the first people to spearhead programs to develop theories in sports.
Zhang Shan	She became the first woman to win the mixed skeet shooting event at the Olympics, in Barcelona, Spain, in 1992. She scored 223 hits, equalling the men's world mark.
Zheng Xiaoying	China's first woman conductor, she is senior conductor with the Central Opera Theater in Beijing. Trained in Russia, she founded, together with 17 other women musicians, an all-woman philharmonic chamber orchestra in 1990.
Zhu Mufei	(b. 1897) She became the first woman military pilot in China in 1922. She learned flying from General Zhang Huichang, one of the founders of the Chinese air force. She gained a reputation for bravery in the air force.

Glossary

ancestor worship Sacrifices made to ancestors in order to ensure them a happy afterlife. Ancestral sacrifices could only be made by male descendants.

arranged marriage Marriage arranged by parents, through a go-between or a matchmaker. Children whose marriages are arranged have no say at all over the choice of spouse. Arranged marriages still occur in the countryside.

betrothal gifts Gifts from a man's family to a woman's family after a marriage match has been agreed to by both families.

clan A group comprising a number of households whose heads claim descent from a common ancestor. In China, there are clan villages whose residents all share the same family name.

county town The main town of a county. A county is a rural administrative unit.

Cultural Revolution Initiated by Mao Zedong in 1966; Chinese were asked to rebel against old ideas, old culture, old habits, and old customs. A period of disorder and destruction which ended with the death of Mao in 1976.

extended family A multi-generation family living under one roof. Today, the extended family is more likely a network of related families that maintain very close ties and provide mutual support, but live apart from each other.

filial piety Faithfulness to duty and obligations toward one's parents. Very important in Chinese culture. Children were, and still are, expected to take care of their parents in their old age, and to defer to them.

Great Leap Forward A campaign launched in 1959 to attain national self-sufficiency economically. It had disastrous results, with people suffering from starvation and malnutrition throughout the country due to food shortage.

matrilineal society A society in which descent is traced through the maternal line.

May Seventh Cadre School A special school in the countryside where government employees and intellectuals were sent to work with and learn from the peasants.

patriarchal society A society in which descent is traced through the male line and the father is the supreme authority in the family.

People's Communes These were set up in 1958 in the countryside, the aim of which was to use labor effectively. The People's Communes took over government at the district level, directing what was to be produced and assigning work. They are now being broken up as they have been found unproductive.

prefecture An administrative unit that is a subdivision of the province. It is further divided into counties.

Red Guards They wre militant students who supported Mao's Cultural Revolution. They went on a rampage of destruction in the name of the Revolution.

township An administrative unit in China consisting of a cluster of villages and the surrounding land.

warlord A military commander exercising civil power by force in a limited area.

work unit A general term given to a person's workplace. The large corporations, factories and government institutions generally provide subsidized housing, medical care and education for the workers and their families.

Further Reading

Ayscough, Florence: *Chinese Women: Yesterday and Today*, Da Capo Press, New York, 1975.
Croll, Elizabeth: *The Politics of Marriage in Contemporary China*, Cambridge University Press, New York, 1981.
Croll, Elizabeth, ed.: *China's One-Child Family*, St. Martin's Press, New York, 1985.
Foster, Leila and Nien Cheng: *Courage in China*, Childrens Press, Chicago, 1992.
Headland, I.: *Home Life in China*, Gordon Press, New York, 1972.
Honig, Emily and Hershatter, Gail: *Personal Voices: Chinese Women in the 1980s*, Stanford University Press, Stanford, CA, 1991.
Lin, Alice: *Grandmother Had No Name*, China Books, San Francisco, 1988.
Li Yu-Ning, ed.: *Chinese Women Through Chinese Eyes*, M.E. Sharpe, New York, 1975.
Lin Yu-T'ang: *Widow, Nun, and Courtesan: Three Noveletes from the Chinese*, Greenwood Press, Westport, CT, 1971.
Lo, Ruth E. and Kudeman, Katherine S.: *In the Eye of the Typhoon: An American Woman in China During the Cultural Revolution*, Da Capo Press, New York, 1987.
O'Hara, Albert R.: *The Position of Women in Early China: According to the Lieh Nu Chuan, "Biographies of Eminent Chinese Women,"* Hyperion Press, Westport, CT, 1984.
Pruitt, Ida: *Old Madam Yin: A Memoir of Peking Life*, Stanford University Press, Stanford, CA, 1979.
Thomson, Peggy: *City Kids in China*, Harper and Row, New York, 1991.
Wu Yung: *The Flight of an Empress*, Hyperion Press, Westport, CT, 1985.
Yao, Esther S. Lee: *Chinese Women: Past and Present*, Ide House, Mesquite, TX, 1983.
Zhang Jie: *As Long as Nothing Happens, Nothing Will*, Grove Press, New York, 1991.
————: *Heavy Wings*, Grove Press, New York, 1989.
————: *Love Must Not Be Forgotten*, China Books, San Francisco, 1986.
Zhang Xinxin and Sang Ye: *Chinese Lives: An Oral History of Contemporary China*, Penguin Books, New York, 1986.

Index

PHOTO CREDITS